T0164546

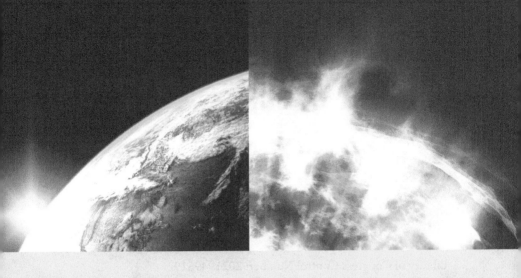

Technofascism

THE NEW WORLD DISORDER

Joel Kabakov PhD

Published by:
Trine Day LLC
PO Box 577
Walterville, OR 97489
1-800-556-2012
www.TrineDay.com
trineday@icloud.com

Library of Congress Control Number: 2021949519

Kabakov, Joel
Technofascism: The New World Disorder—1st ed.
p. cm.

Epub (ISBN-13) 978-1-63424-391-9
Print (ISBN-13) 978-1-63424-390-2
1. Technological innovations -- Social aspects. 2. Technological innovations --
Psychological aspects. 3. Technology -- Philosophy. 4. Technology and civilization. 5. Science -- Psychological aspects. 6. Poetry. I. Kabakov, Joel II. Title

First Edition
10 9 8 7 6 5 4 3 2 1

Distribution to the Trade by:
Independent Publishers Group (IPG)
814 North Franklin Street
Chicago, Illinois 60610
312.337.0747
www.ipgbook.com

Publisher's Foreword

What do you do with the defective slaves?

What do you do with the defective slaves?
Do you set them aside?
Do you boil them in oil?
Do you deceive them,
As, you bleed them,
All the while?

What do you do with the defective slaves?
Do you get them to fight one another?
To save you the bother?
Now, you lose,
By the way,
Everytime;
But the play is the game,
And it ain't always the same.
And isn't being a player,
Better than,
Being the game?

What do you do with the defective slaves?
Effectively, cajoling away,
Away down the river,
Away till the time,
A will and a way,
For the defective slaves.

Onward to the utmost of futures.
Peace
RA Kris Millegan
Publisher
TrineDay
January 19, 2022

Contents

Foreword

Philosophy questions, while Poetry speaks. And how, in this world, we hunger for one crumb of direct, salt speech, for the potency and freshness toward which Orwell bids us in his "Politics and the English Language." For Raymond Barfield "Poetry is primal, formal, finished," whereas Philosophy, within which I include Computer Science, is "belated, open, skeptical, unfinished, and difficult."

In my teaching of "Digital Self Defence" and "Ethics for Hackers" I have stumbled awkwardly on a lonely, frustrating path toward civic cyber-security, unable to reach a generation alienated from technology to which they are helplessly enslaved.

A chorus of concerned scientists now raise their voices. The likes of Sir Tim Berners Lee are not Luddites nor wildmen in woodland shacks foaming against science, but those who love, and have given their lives to technology only to see it co-opted, by what? ... We do not find the words. They are not like us.

As computer scientists we are drowning, not merely in technical complexity, but in a moral mire. Our creations turned against us, betrayed by corporations, government intelligence agencies, advertisers and demagogues. How are we to find the words of warning, of protest, and of hope?

Words expire, as Nietzsche said, like old coins whose faces wear smooth. "Efficiency," in the words of mathemetician and digital artist Miller Puckette, is overrated. "Correctness," as Neil Postman reminded us, is parochial arrogance. We are slaves to unqualified abstract nouns, who forgot to ask... "progress" toward what? "Connectedness" to whom? Security for whom, from who, and to what end? In our "Age of the Unthinkable," Joshua Cooper Ramo surmises, as more recently does security engineer Bruce Schniere, that human needs for long term security, for democracy, freedom and happiness can no longer be serviced by efficient, convenient machines. And in our hearts we all know this.

Yet here is Joel Kabakov, with the convenient efficiency of the poet's pen. His word is "Technofascism." Fresh. Provocative. Timely.

While we were asking "reasonable and balanced" questions, Poetry spoke. Technofascism is here. Coming from neither the political left nor right, the transformation of our beloved technology into tyranny seems to be a global and universal process. Does something within us crave enslavement and the beatings of a harsh mechanical master? Is the abdication of human will to a new religion? Is Silicon Valley a promised land, or dark cult?

And if Kabakov's word is a call to arms, as our grandfathers who fought fascism, we must now ask not if "Technology can save us?," but if "We can save technology?"

Andy Farrell
Author of Digital Vegan, Applied Scientific Press 2021

ANACRUSIS

WHITE CLOUDS

"Technological progress is like an axe in the hands of a pathological criminal."
— A. Einstein

Hollywood could not have gotten it better: white clouds parting over the pastoral town of Guernica in Northern Spain on a brilliant afternoon in April 1937, revealing the gleaming wings of the German Condor Legion flying in perfect formation, about to deliver their deadly payloads on an unsuspecting population below, an historic first. This lurid scene not only sets the stage for the first large-scale coordinated aerial bombing in history, but conjures a working prototype of the waging of war in the coming age, the age of technofascism. In a wider aperture, the *a priori* role of science and technology as life supportive are about to fall into enemy hands.

The sheer collaborative treachery between Spain's Franco and Hitler serves as sinister prelude to World War II, wherein air power was anticipated to be the most efficient way for the axis to attack enemy held territory with utmost deadly precision: death delivered from a distance. Flesh and blood are about to become blips and specks.

In utter synchronicity, the most renowned Spanish painter of the day, Pablo Picasso, had just been commissioned by the 1937 Paris International Arts Exposition to produce a major new work. Upon hearing of the horrific bombings, the artist produced, virtually overnight, the mural sized painting, "Guernica," considered one of the premier masterpieces of protest art of all time.[1] The sensation swirling around this work exhibited at the Expo attracted a Gestapo officer who shouted in Picasso's face, "who did this?" to which the master rejoined, "you did"!

Monarchs historically rule Empires. Julius Caesar was a perfect match for Rome; no need to relinquish power to the senate except as a display of sham democracy that was never meant to materialize. Aqueducts and highways were not only magnificent "technologies antiques," but were achievements without which the Empire might be untenable.

Then came the deadly coup. Of course the empire survived with new dictatorial blood at the helm. Such assorted monarchs discover sooner or later that the greater the geographic reach of empire, the greater the need for social control at home accompanied by brutal state crackdowns on dissent no matter how just or popular. In fact, the mass projection of power abroad requires a massive labor class at home, the one most likely to give rise to humanitarian protest movements. Hence, support for the emperor-dictator necessitates more than a matter of collective consent; it absolutely requires that everyone serve the state whether directly or indirectly. Subsequently, through the ages, in empire states "e tu" New York!- any collective desire for liberty and the right of dissent has been drummed out of the populous by hook or by crook whenever it arises thereby keeping any glimmer of democracy in political eclipse. Good morning America.

Monotheism and monarchy share more than just four letters of the alphabet. They shared "one God" religious paradigm among Jew, Christian and Muslim presents yet an additional set of problems to the spirit and institution of democracy. For despite the separation of church and state as constitutional principle we cannot expect individuals to relinquish their belief that the universe is essentially a monarchy under God. Applied to politics, even subconsciously, "down ballot" elected officials are no more than lower-archic paper shufflers and bloviators at best, divinely created to serve the empire and its primate. So imprinted into the deep psyche of modern societies are pseudo-ordained hierarchies, that concepts such as "created equal" are obviated even as religious practice and participation fall out of fashion.

Now technology wants to have it both ways….it wants to be, through its potentates, church and state, elevated to a religion but at the same time, the leading edge of classical science. Evidence for this lies all around us: man–in-space religion ; total surveillance state equated with divine omniscience, bioengineering = divine afflatus, war's mega death and destruction as holy crusades. And of course there's the lottery, numbers drive destiny.

Need I point out the flaws in the above missions in a world in which billions go to bed -if they own a bed- hungry? The abandonment of science and technology and peer enforced ethics as the coin of the realm for the alleviation of human suffering, is high on the short list of greatest betrayals in the history of "developed nations." At the same time a new quasi-Jungian personality type emerges which is brutal on the inside and foolish or benign on the outside. This fits as perfect dramatis personae into Hannah Arendt's trope, "the banality of evil."[2]

A core objective of the technofascist state is the creation of a proxy culture that replaces and eventually destroys culture itself. The new industrial revolution around technology requires a work force that abandons personal history at the door to the office, the factory, the computer screen, the gun turret, the check out counter and even the gas pump. Hence the argument that in a white patriarchal society, at least we have the freedom to keep our cultural heritage alive is tested if not obviated. "I am the first member of my family who went to college" can form a meme whose ultimate effect is to challenge Dr. King's maxim that a man be judged by the content of his character when, in fact, that college student becomes the bank officer foreclosing on members of one's own cultural community as a more-than-willing instrument of economic oppression. Along with the perception of overcoming racism in the work place comes a kind of ethical "free pass" wherein a person of color for example, has risen from oppressed to oppressor with "risen" being the operative principle. This establishes an existential dichotomy in the meaning of success in toto both materially and spiritually as well as an opportunity for people and institutions to exploit ethnicity as a kind of fabricated humanism. The United States gets its first black president, first chairman of the Joint Chiefs, first Secretary of State and so on. Identification with the oppressor is nothing new but cultural self-eradication is rising to new heights under the guise of diversity in the workplace.

Concurrently, we may realize that the struggle to empower women and other gender based struggles are chronically co-opted through tokenism and partial fixes. Was the women's movement ever meant to populate positions of power in a patriarchy? Or was it conceived as a way to overturn the patriarchy itself? No one is asking for perfection yet today equality means little more than a slow walked exercise-en-route.

In America, an abundance of presidents of both parties, and their respective administrations, who have advanced a mythical technological paradigm, beg for full- voiced inclusion in any comprehensive history of the United States and the "developed" world. Here we have one of the most ironclad arguments against the tenuous, permeable membrane that separates our two establishment parties. Capitalistic progress and innovation are immune to party politics and nearly immune to elections themselves. Just consider the corporate campaign donors who give to both sides of an election contest.

There is no set formula for how and when a modern constitutional democracy devolves toward empire. The classical Romans had never dreamt of a corporate state where politicians swayed to the beat of transnational elites. One way or the other, we live in a time of titular democratic societies tending to gravitate toward autocratic heads of state in apparent contradiction to their own political DNA.

Meanwhile concerned citizens fulminate over Citizens United, Wall Street bailouts, deadly drone strikes, police racism, immigration sweeps et al. In flawed response, many retain their belief in a political pendulum swing that is sure to favor humanitarian values in the next election. Yet, if there existed an underlying dynamic which allowed democracies to self correct over time, we wouldn't need a discourse on technofascism.

Great works of fiction often sport marquee titles like "The Sound and the Fury" and "East of Eden." While it's not good literary etiquette for an author to dub his own title a great one, any book the likes of Technofascism begs a reckoning between pretense and substance. And while this book is nonfiction it speaks to a plethora of fictions with which mankind have surrounded themselves as we collectively permit false progress to approach the event horizon, and hence, suck us all into oblivion.

Surely we inflicted this sad subject upon ourselves just as we brought on Picasso's salutary Guernica in witness to that infamous technofascist terror carpet-bombing of a civilian population by the evil Condor Legion.

The real meaning of regime change must be, as prefigured in the Declaration of Independence, the people rising up and defeating tyranny in their own government no matter how powerful or sacrosanct .

Indeed, humankind has chronically failed to heed the words of President Eisenhower who while in office, witnessed the resources of a "great nation" usurped by the military industrial complex, bringing about the permanent war economy which has, in the ensuing half century, tightened its strangle hold on American resources both material and spiritual.

Nor have we heeded Arthur C Clark and Stanley Kubrick who got it right in 2001 A Space Odyssey, wherein the Odyssean battle with Cyclops reincarnates in Hal, a cybernetic incubus who engages in a death struggle with humanity itself. Such an epic takes its place in the canon of technofascism.

I have squandered all too many years spouting rejoinders every time my wife laments the downfall of mankind beginning with the invention of the wheel. Granted, the only wheel in Native American culture was the medicine wheel and the quality of life certainly did not improve for them with the torrent of technologies that came out of industrial Europe. God bless the medicine wheel.

One need not to hold so radical a view to see how technology and power have left Faust in the dust in terms of unholy alliances. Taste the GMO food, breathe the irradiated air, take a dip in dioxin-laced water or awaken to the renewed interest in the use of nuclear weapons to face future wars, acting in concert with pure fascist doctrine requiring a general degradation of society, disempowerment of the individual and the humane organizations to which he subscribes, all in turn under the reign of a de facto dictator.

Like it or not technofascism is here. It arrived while our species wasn't looking. We were staring at our screens, driving our cars, punching in and out at work and consuming the gadgets and innovations that knocked us off-task of responsible citizenship. Meanwhile, the predators were all running full tilt with high tech weapons of mass exploitation. It takes not a Freud to tell us that technology has given rise to the greatest sense of false empowerment the world over since perhaps the invention of gunpowder. Be first on your block to use yet another new word: technipotence. So let's look hard at this new blunderbuss we have come up with before it backfires in our collective face.

The now infamous raid on the capital on 1/6 which was far too organized and pre-planned to be considered a spontaneous riot, could not have been carried out without a number of assault teams, each with their own weaponized communications network.

This may backfire on us all by hastening a number of laws impacting the entire activist spectrum from left to right and the social media that support it.

How Shall We Dress for Nuclear Winter?

How shall we dress darling, for nuclear winter?
shall we wear scarves woven from the clasped fingers
of pilgrims at prayer?

shall we choose from a thousand abandoned overalls
strewn on the floor of the bomb factory at the edge of
town?
shall we protect our eyes with glamorous goggles gone
opaque,
refusing the trickle of photons from an obscure sun?
or just stay in our florid pajamas today
tip-toeing from the kitchen to the parlor
worried about a likelihood of burnt toast?

how shall we dress darling?
our boots are rated to below zero
perfect for the new zero of extinction

we are in good company
thunder lizards of the cretaceous
en-famed in the great halls of science

what goes good with this bulletproof vest?
what matches my military helmet?
a mustard seed in glass around my neck?
ear buds blaring the hardest of rock?

the clock is frozen at two minutes to midnight.
the faucet in the kitchen drips

I fasten my watch to my wrist
preparing to go about my business,
reminiscing of sundials,
an inkling of breezes
and the lost epic of spring.

1

A Constellation of Death Stars

We shape our tools and afterwards, our tools shape us"
– Marshall Mcluhan

Homo Sapiens Sapiens is an idiosyncratic species that presents a constellation of contradictory behaviors: a love of custom and tradition with its veneration for ancestors, patriarchs, august governing bodies et al, in juxtaposition to innovation, counter-instinctual behaviors, pyramid building, space travel, extreme technologies. Even upon learning through experience that some of these behaviors and devices that race far beyond the basic desiderata of survival are not constructive in the least, that they pollute the environment, terrorize the innocent, promulgate new cancers to replace the ones finally cured, our beloved species is wont to live in denial of its self-devolution. It's as if all circumspection is lost in the fast shuffle of neat ideas that inflame the minds of the perpetrators like a gambler at craps just knowing that the next roll will redeem a game that keeps breaking even at best.

Science at best, listens ... and wonders, correcting its course through consensus, experimentation, verification and prediction. Technology can be the enemy of science by fabricating devices like nuclear power plants, that co-opt scientific ethics and vision, while camouflaging risk, all for a quick return on investment.

Few contemporary scientists among us are willing to consider that shoddy science fixed by better science may be best fixed by no science at all. That is why the biotech industry persists even after GMO's are shown to have negative health consequences. It is axiomatic that good science fixes bad science, lest the inventor of the new improved nipple discovers that breast-feeding is best.

The advent of rudderless science may be traced to the bifurcation between philosophy and science in the mid nineteenth century. Only Freud and perhaps Marx attempted to preserve the union of the two only to be inundated by the flood of technology and industrial élan that crescendo to this day. Indeed a good philosopher peeking over Oppenheimer's shoulder during the Manhattan Project seems like a good idea. What is it that we hear about weaponizing space? Dirty bombs anyone? What is it that we hear about new psychogenic drugs that will make us feel competent or attentive....even loved? Freud in his firmament is appalled.

Technofascism is the unbridled development of technologies as extensions of collective human power both political and entrepreneurial in amassing capital, military dominance, dominating markets, institutions and natural resources. It is developed and practiced across borders and continents and fiscal years such that no state can effectively regulate it, limit it or degrade it. It enjoys as its operatives some of the brightest and most enterprising minds, which, having fallen under the mystical spell of technology, simply fail to view themselves as playing high and fast with the future of humanity. For they are enrolled in the school of building progress with ever greater progress, arms with deadlier arms, megabytes with gigabytes. This always ends in negatively offsetting any benefit to the greater good of the population. Fortunately, unlike a military campaign, such a business model cannot be veiled in secrecy for long. Yet the shenanigans proceed apace in the form of diversionary proxy wars, foreign political meddling at all levels, graft and corruption; in short, the whole technofascist tool box. Little wonder that this new ideology has captured the imaginations and ambitions of politicians and heads of state.

Back in the day, the late thirties, it was IBM cardpunch technology that enabled the Nazis to perform thorough demographics on virtually all cities and towns in Germany pursuant to rounding up undesirables and sending them out to concentration camps. Jews, gypsies and some other minorities were all identified and located as part of the program.

"Big Blue" as IBM is affectionately known on Wall Street has never looked back. For the Nazis to deploy Big Blue with banal efficiency targeting the ethnicity and religion of innocent human beings speaks to a monstrous pathology manifested as a complete loss of empathy for human life itself.[1] The appalling, and underreported, support for the Third Reich by highly placed financiers and industrialists in America is a nauseating subject that we have yet to face full on, even now in the new millennium.

World War II was the first war whose outcome was decided by truly "facile" technology-based killing from great distances with bombs, rockets and nuclear devices. What better living example of Hegel's idea of alienation.

Don't fire until you see their blips on the radar screen, until you hear their engines on the sonar, until you intercept their electrical communications over the wire. This led to a staggering array of extreme devices, which took war from one-on-one scale to a mass destructive force that redefined the nature of human conflict forever. Yet the allure of technology lead the military to doggedly believe that for every lethal device there was an equal and opposite defense, armor, anti-missile etc. . Hence the expected –nay, desired- realization that we should all disarm was always muttered with forked tongue, while new technologies rolled off the assembly line climaxing in the cold war itself. Those who remain until this day defiant of the Geneva Conventions, The Nuremburg principles, The United Nations Charter and articles are nothing more that Technofascists. Try and stop them we must.

Major enablers of the technofascist agenda are those who believe we can simultaneously benefit humanity by building our stock portfolios as we advocate for unions, garment industries, the control of natural resources in the developing world, child labor, prison labor and portfolios stuffed with high interest debt. And all this is somehow made tolerable by its a-tactile remoteness, much like the media sanitizing war reportage-how do you spell dereliction?

Technofascist magnates of whom there are legion view everything through a technological lens. When a company has had a bad year or even a bad quarter, a dedicated computer spreadsheet is generated that tells management just which and how many jobs need to be furloughed or terminated in order to hold stock values steady. In other words, as legions of workers are laid off, Wall Street and its media stooges put a positive spin on it all by emphasizing the rescuing of the corporation as if it were a child down a well. All this while allowing our hard earned pension funds to devalue to farthings on the dollar.

Such practices engender a split personality, so to speak in the American economy between the general welfare as contained in the constitution and capitalist dogma which exploit and divide the population in the building of financial and industrial institutions, that is, until we the people finally become *we the shareholders* and *we the members of the board*.

While the former mandates elected politicians there is an increasing trend for them to serve the latter, that is, with the ascendancy of lobbying. Every time a member of congress commits to lunch with a corporate lobbyist they no doubt go out to their favorite death star cantina to discuss the next heist.

There are no greater occupiers of the language than silver-tongued presidents of the United States. After a lot of head jerking from teleprompter

13

to teleprompter, have we heard a speech by its true author? While it's easy to hold up Mr. Trump as a poseur-in-chief of pulp tabloid content, there is no excuse for his predecessor using his pulpit to systematically reverse many of his campaign positions- much to the delight of the deep state overlords-, which inevitably impact deep issues at the heart of his political party.

A partial list of post election Obama fails: Lack of proper prosecution of those responsible for the BP Gulf oil spill and other environmental abuses, failure to push for a non-corporate controlled health care act with public option or single payer, an unfulfilled promise to end U.S. involvement in Afghanistan and other armed conflicts in the region, stalled efforts for championing lasting peace and justice for Israel and Palestine, failure to curtail mammoth arms sales to Saudi Arabia, no promised reduction of the over 700 billion in defense spending, failed closing of Gitmo, flubbed rescue of Flint residents, failed cancellation of Dakota Access Ppipeline (an environmental menace), along with greatly diminishing all fossil fuel extraction, an end to drastic meddling in election integrity abroad, waffling on the strengthening and chastening of the U.S. position on climate change, reversed build down of the nuclear weapons arsenal by means of a "modernization" to the tune of a trillion dollars, half-hearted launching of a massive energy infrastructure build featuring post greenhouse energy, pro-active community policing programs and accountability systems for brutal practices, a truly equitable path to citizenship and an end to mass deportations of non-criminal immigrants and asylum seekers, net neutrality, cessation of Wall Street bailouts and prosecution of Wall Street robber barons, opposition to the NSA tapping into communications data of all citizens in tandem with the Defense Authorization act wherein any citizen can be held indefinitely without charge, a ban on GMOs, a ban on glyphosate based insecticides, enforcement of fuel economy and pollution standards for vehicles and heavy industry, reform of predatory student debt financing practices as well as the general unaffordability of higher education, mandating minimum wage programs nationally, a voluntary end –for Democrats at least- of super PAC and pay to play money in politics and neither last nor least, a verifiable, auditable election ballot system. [2]

...Were you holding your breath? If so you just set a Guinness record.
Are Ralph Nader and other critics of our present two-party system
right by calling them one big duopoly?

For those who point out that our Obama-defeating congress committed legislative obstruction unopposed need look a bit further. Well documented historically is the countervailing power of executive orders in synch with a President's ability to spearhead his own political will toward mounting a successful campaign with vast popular support at his back. This is where Obama simply dribbled the clock out. Where were the three-pointers when we needed them? We can have scholarly discourse all day long about American economic history, but the incontrovertible reality is that the under-classes, under-employed, undereducated of all races and ages are rhetorically finessed by insidious politicians into helping them win elections, only to be routinely abandoned on day two by monolithic corrupt capitalist practices hard wired up and down the entire economy.

All this would not be possible without a pervasive technology savvy data controlling network which is programmed to know just what to let in, what to keep in and what and when to disseminate.

$$m = \iiint\limits_{(V)} \rho(x, y, z) \, dV$$

$$D = ?$$

$$\int_e dy$$

$$\int dz$$

$$D = x = a/\varepsilon$$

$$\frac{e^x y^2}{x^2}$$

$$x^3(x$$

$$ax^2 + $$

$$a\left(x + \frac{1}{2}\right.$$

$$(\ln/u)' = \frac{u'}{u}$$

$$\sqrt[5]{5}$$

$$\sin($$

$$m)(\ln)$$

$$\frac{\sin(x-1)}{x}$$

$$u = N \cdot \frac{3}{2} K P T;$$

2

CHAOS BY DESIGN

"The best way to unleash chaos is to demand order"
=JK

G rowing up in a borderline kosher household with erratically observed customs in the kitchen; I could now and then be seen running through the house with a glass of milk, my father storming after me with half Yiddish threats because I served myself a dairy drink with a "fleishig" (meat) meal. This taught me a keen sense of chaotic household management: on-again, off-again enforcement but always keeping you off balance and guessing whether you lived in a free or authoritarian regime. That same father figure keeps you on a "need to know" basis, essentially in the dark about what really goes on in the world, obscuring what particular issue or moral nuance is possessing him in the moment.

Nations do not solve problems in the spectacle of media any more than pornography contributes to healthy fertility in a population. It is the slam-bang effect of everything that attracts major media production more and more in the present generation. The media still stand on the shoulders of William Randolph Hearst who said, "you furnish the pictures and I'll furnish the war."[1] And now with the sensational archiving and editing tools augmented by shallow tabloid style narrative, high rise buildings fall down, cities drown, bombs burst in churches, black lives are snuffed out and as many acquire a, somewhat detached distance from the horrid content.

That very observation should lead to a healthy disdain for the media campaigns as conducted by political parties, branches of the government, the armed forces and their corporate partners –in- mayhem. Yet save the true critical and creative souls among us who rise to question the major media and its purveyors of sound and fury, the situation is worsening by the day. Donald Trump has found a match between his successful management style which wastes no opportunity for all "in the room" to be thrown off balance and into a world defined by his wreckless use of authority resulting in agendas remaining crumpled in coat pockets amid fears of displeasing the monarch flailing before them.

The 2016 electoral primary season was locked in the thrall of two personalities: Donald Trump and Bernie Sanders. All things being on the level in the media, as a generation ago when equal media coverage was enforced by the FCC, there would have certainly been a fifty-fifty allotment of time and commentary to these individuals with Hillary coming in a close third and the sad lot of remaining contenders coming in fourth. So what brought on the chaos in reportage? Where were the decisions made? How did chaos-making play a role in the election? Be it known without question that Bernie is anathema to technofascism. He reinstates a nurturing, humanistic approach to governance. Given the choice between a genuine champion of the people and a drone of the techno t-rexes, say no more .

Give Bernie proportionate coverage and there goes our anchor sponsors; goodbye petro dollars, Monsanto dollars, Merrill Lynch dollars, Johnson and Johnson dollars et al.

This looming threat brought chaos to the production teams at the cables and the networks, not only to the candidate race but to vital stories like climate change, poverty in America, and to coverage of election inequities themselves: voter suppression, Bernie suppression, third party suppression, suppression, suppression, suppression. And into the tabloid news-talk rooms rush our smack down panels of talking heads, the pseudo right seesawing with the faux left or worse yet the hyper-slanted anchors, the Maddows , the Hannitys et al.

The etiology of right wing rulership emanates from the patriarchal dictator-father model. Rather than dismissing it we need to juxtapose it with participatory democracy, contrast the two and come up with an analysis of why the American electorate periodically elevates one over the other. It seems that the competing archetypes of heads of state globally are contained in two constructs: rulership and leadership.

Once the general population is attracted to a ruler figure it is a given that they have opted to relinquish their own right of liberty, equality and brotherhood installing in their stead a pseudo hierarchic empowerment focusing on enemies without and within. What is worse, the ruler now has the power to launch a war "on behalf" of all of his subjects as could be the case with Donald Trump and Kim Jan Il. Two matching autocrats like peas in a pod, but given the power gap between them, which is the greater bully? It should be pure paradox that an extreme authoritarian wins the popular vote in an election. Somewhere in my archives I have a picture of a medical doctor on a poster endorsing filter cigarettes.

Need one mention that surely, no conflict between the North Korean people and the Americans has ever existed? Yet those who rule have buried this pesky fact beneath a pile of propaganda. War making and democracy are antipodes.

In the mid nineteen eighties, the great philosopher and educator, Jiddu Krishnamurti delivered open-air talks in an oak grove in Ojai California. My wife and I were in the audience for several of them. His speech was eloquent, serene and penetrating. In one of these talks he began to descant on the word *bully*, repeating it in a long list such as: religious bullies, political bullies, educational bullies and financial bullies and on and on. Why so monochrome a use of language? As in poetry, parallelism is a great way of making your point. Beside living in a world in which bullies are in the ascendant class, the bully is a fundamental personality type in the authoritarian model of rulership. We don't necessarily like the bully but we fear him/her and want his approval just like the boss at work or a dictatorial dad at the dinner table, the judgmental priest or the stern "schulmeister" of a teacher.

At present in the American political scene, prominent ex-political leaders are almost nowhere to be seen. You would expect the Bushes to be constantly in front of microphones and the press and town halls pitching the so-called conservative view of things. And where are the Obamas, Clintons, pitching their cause? Where are they all? I suspect that "duck and cover" is making a come back.

Jeremy Corbyn is indeed the leader of the opposition in England and is all over the media on a daily basis. Hey guys, what are you running from? Maybe it's in anticipation of the demise of the American two party system itself.

As for the rulership/leadership dichotomy, Great Britain sorted that out uneventfully in the nineteenth century with the parliamentary system by converting the monarchy to figure head status. In contrast, the United States oscillates between the two models with Lincoln having attributes of both. When Lincoln pivoted from Civil War victory to the Indian wars in the west, a puff of black smoke emerged from his stovepipe hat and he never looked back. One of the greatest body counts of Native Americans occurred under the Lincoln presidency. Fact. This cemented Lincoln's dualistic legacy.[2] It has become abundantly clear that the Democratic National Committee is practicing its own style of management through chaos. Try as they might, the TV production teams at the 2020 Philadelphia nominating convention could not keep the obvious turmoil coming from podium as well as the floor, off the screen. The sit-ins at the media tent by citizens joined by delegates is but one example. Also, we would have had a much fairer and democratic –pun intended- proceeding had the super delegates not moved in like an invading hoard. To think that the notorious practice of voter roll stripping occurred through collusion between the DNC and their New York organization boggles the mind. Après pos Florida, Fox News accurately stated, "The case being heard in a Florida courtroom dates back to last summer, when the Democrats were thrown into turmoil following the leak of documents that appeared to show some DNC officials conspiring to undermine Sanders in the party primary. Jared Beck, a Harvard law expert, shortly afterward filed a class-action lawsuit on behalf of residents of 45 states against the DNC and former chairwoman Debbie Wasserman Schultz."[3]While the charges were summarily dismissed in a Florida courtroom, they were never strongly contested by the DNC.

So now the big "D" joins the big "R" in election rigging. So called caging, the work of Crosscheck corporation, gerrymandering and every manner of making free and fair elections an impossible dream are now in play across the country. For the DNC to go through two disgraced chairs in election season sets a new record. Do the research, preferably online.

One area where Mr. Trump wins the king of chaos award hands down, is in disaster response. You thought Bush 43 and "Brownie" took the cake during Katrina in '05. Well say hello to Donald J Trump who is already out-stalling 43 on hurricane Maria as she tops fifty billion in recovery and rebuilding efforts. So the power wielding tyrant of the hour now ironically embodies the dark Reagan quote, "government is not the solution to our problem, government is the problem."[4]

Gazing up at the starry sky, we initially see a somewhat random configuration of stars, the moon, clouds and maybe a couple of planets. In minutes the patterns begin to emerge, Orion's belt, the Northern Cross, Sirius cradled in the moon's scimitar across the sky. The longer and deeper we look and the more we study the more patterning we see. The human mind makes patterns of everything, even its own history. It follows logically that chaos consists largely of natural phenomena that don't seem to conform to human pattern making or simply remain beyond the comprehension of the mind. Astronomers tell us that the largest galaxies hold as many as a trillion stars. Now that's a trillion things all agreeing to rotate around a nucleus in disk formation every few light years. Does gravity and motion explain that magnitude of cosmic consensus? I think not; but what I do sense is that there is a less documented force at play in the universe which I call, "the force of pattern."

People who never look mindfully at the cosmos are just as hard wired as astronomers in seeing the patterns in almost everything from human behavior to calendars to politics. There is little tolerance in human nature for chaos though it might fall into consensus minutes later. A likely outcome of this is that the imposition of pattern and order, especially to the extreme can be destructive to order itself. Those in positions of authority who enforce order so easily cross the line into blatant aggression with few –along with the perpetrator- noticing the shift in the least. What is more, those who oppose aggression with reason, with free speech, with an arsenal of ironclad truth are bound to be put down in the mismatch between gentle and forceful approaches.

3

SUNKEN SHIPS DON'T LEAK

"Peace is bad for business"

– J.K.

ockroaches know they are not welcome a split second after the light goes on in the kitchen. But the jig is already up. It doesn't matter where they hide. A really good and appropriate leaker is first and foremost a whistle blower. He's the guy who turns the light on in the kitchen. The most important history book never written would be "History's Greatest Whistle Blowers" available at libraries and school rooms and Greyhound Bus Station racks in your neighborhood.

Keeping the name Julian Assange out of the first paragraph of this chapter was a Herculean feat. It is *his* ears that are ringing from the flood of dedicated truth tellers, the rare dispensers of vaccines into the pathogenic capillaries of the technofascist anatomy.

Where would we now be without the revelations of Manning, Snowden, Assange qua Wikileaks and Drake? But more importantly, how have the monumental Pentagon Papers of Ellsberg a generation ago not led to a thorough national self examination followed at last by the vaunted increase in transparency as promised by Obama during his stunning campaign for president? But alas, here we are, inundated by unhinged invective coming from all sides whose interlocutors keep us distracted from the truth.

When the first order of business every day is to crank out talking points, place bullying calls to media executives, write tendentious Op Eds, go on scripted talk shows and vociferate in righteous decibels about border security, Russian hacking and other tabloid pulp you know you are a political animal riding a boat that is already half way down to Davy Jones' locker. But that fact seems to have little affect on you or the political party establishment in this country.

When you insist on clinging to a sunken boat, leaks and whistle blowing cease having any affect. The concept of Public Relations in a technofascist context translates to control of language, printed, broadcast and on the web through complex search engine censorship. This forms the foundation of a chain of information that coerces speech, thought and social behavior. Both the first Gulf war and the Iraq war were developed as massive public relations campaigns sold to the people by the likes of George Bush senior, Colin Powell and Tony Blair.[1]

The system of international justice has yet to make the equation between the use of rhetoric to create wars and prosecutable criminal conspiracy. And all with the help of Nancy Pelosi who by creating the trope, "impeachment is off the table" on the reelection of Bush 43, ended up setting justice back while giving a big credibility boost to those in power who shamelessly go on authoring and revising history at will.

Of course the incriminating leaks continue apace but they are simply outshouted by a chorus of technofascist speech writers, journalist shills, patronized pundits, corrupt legal figures and -why blow me down!- educators. Actually, there are instruments of transparency that are law of the land such as FOIA, Freedom of Information Act, which went into affect in 1967 over President Johnson's objections.[2] Federal agencies do reserve the right to redact F.O.I.A. documents with impunity and there is no recourse to dispute their abuse of black ink.

What do you do when the ship of state goes down in a sea of hate? You come up with a whole menu of potential wars, one in Asia, several in the Middle East, one in Eastern Europe and a couple in Africa. That should keep us ahead of news at eleven. In the Federalist Papers, Madison warns founders and incipient citizens of the temptation of a president to use foreign wars as a diversion from domestic strife:

"The means of defence against foreign danger, have been always the instruments of tyranny at home."[3]

Say hello to the Gulf of Tonkin resolution as revealed in Ellsberg's release of the Pentagon Papers. Say hello to 9/11. Meet and greet the stated impending annihilation of North Korea. I mean, what am I missing?

The shear number of FBI informants, some of whom take the bait of convoluted sting operations in which well meaning "good guys" are conveniently turned into fall guys, is gob smacking. The deep seeded language of "conspiracy theorists," coined to hang a label of cultural quackery on anyone who peers behind the curtain of FBI reality manipulation and mendacious intel, paints the popular culture as unworthy of any influence over the state. Face it; terrorist cells are good for business in the world of spy craft and federal law enforcement. And with the New York Times and Washington Post along with the preponderance of mainstream news watching the feds' backs, those pesky web based radical news sites don't stand a chance to break through the corporate media fire wall.

One would hope that the world has its eye on the multimillion dollar agreement between Jeff Bezos, the Washington Post and the CIA as they endeavor- under the pretext of cloud storage- to manipulate messaging and human thought itself having reverse engineered McLuhan and Orwell's sociologies in whole cloth.[4]

ASYLUM

Some wars don't really end
they are plowed under like a ruined crop
whose deadly spores ride out on the airwaves
the same waves that carried the voices of
those who had ruled all along
even when there appeared to be free speech
and lively discourse.

the world of perceptions is on the attack
from outer space and from the end of a spoon.

the real world cowers and stares at the morning paper
forgets what it is eating
partially digesting.

the executioners now practice the social graces
right down to their warm smiles, pertinent words
and rapid-fire speech.

I am at the table
hoping for a morning
a veteran of last night's assault of dreams
telling me that the refugee problem has spread to me
and to the refuge I just attained last Tuesday
after a lifetime of searching.

illusion of stasis while the Earth sends me to
the four corners of the universe.

who is not an asylum seeker?

who is not a castaway from known coordinates
to the unknown?

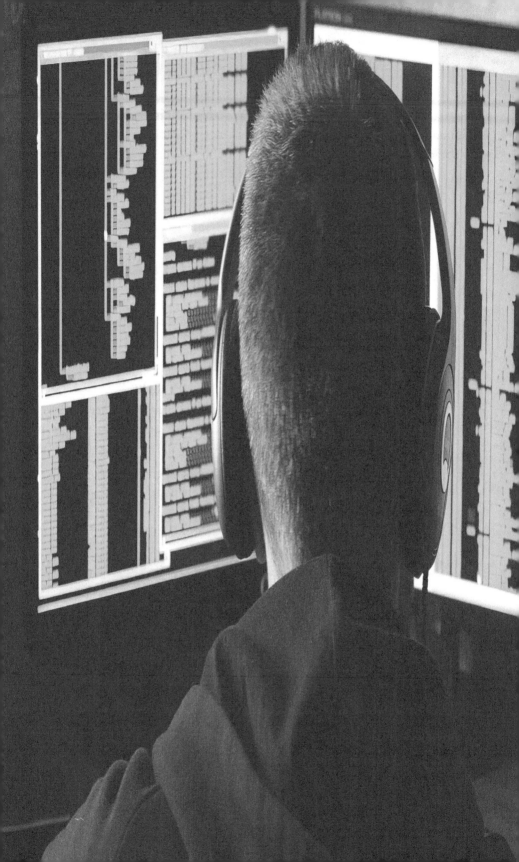

4

ALGORITHMS UBER ALLES

"The more the data banks record about each one of us, the less we exist"
                                                        – Marshall Mcluhan

Computer based day traders, program traders and currency exchange brokers would never think of checking the technofascist party affiliation box next to their names. This is partly due to the fact that the damage they do to the general population is somewhat remote and selectively negligent. Silicon is a virtual sword and shield.

No blood is directly spilled, no shrapnel lying around. But when a market bubble bursts or a huge economic meltdown is triggered by these guys, people who feel it the most are the workers at the companies that go bust or the retirees with limited stock portfolios and on down the line.

Software executives at the New York Stock Exchange are in place at the opening of a typical trading day. It might appear that real people are performing acts that buy and sell shares but computers are racing way ahead, able to accomplish bundles of sales in milliseconds that would take the people days or weeks to accomplish.

It's easy to remark "so what?' to the speed of market trades. But just how rampantly the power of program trading has driven those who converted banks into speculative delivery systems with securitized mortgage instruments bent on wildly risking the investments of millions of home owners all over the country... and the world, is astonishing. And when the artificially inflated sub-prime market burst, guess who paid the bill for the bail out...

In the area of stocks, bonds, securities, commodities futures and to some extent, land and properties, the cyber equivalent to war is occurring continuously. Hand to hand, byte-to-byte combat is the order of the day. This is where a good percentage of technofascist foot soldiers go to virtually fight and die.

In a major article on Wall Street Nick Bauman of Mother Jones wrote several years ago, "Traders' need for speed has grown so voracious that two companies are currently building underwater cables (price tag: around $300 million each) across the Atlantic, in an attempt to join Wall

Street and the London Stock Exchange by the shortest, fastest route possible. One of the cables is expected to shave five to six milliseconds off trans-Atlantic trades. But why stop there? One trading engineer has proposed positioning a line of drones over the ocean, where they would flash microwave data from one to the next like the chain of mountaintop signal fires in The Lord of the Rings. "At what point do you say, 'This is fast enough'?" asks Brent Weisenborn, a former NASDAQ vice president."[1]

There is a striking model for the technofascist financial culture in human health: autoimmune disease. The human body has a network of functions and substances that defend it from disease and disorder from within and without. This is roughly analogous to insuring one's possessions, house, life, car, and profession against loss both natural and man-made. Everyone knows that every so often a house burns down, a homicide is committed in pursuit of a big pay off. When any part of the immune system over-functions, in a sense doesn't know when to stop, you can develop conditions like Crone's disease, Rheumatoid Arthritis and Celiac disease. The result can be systemic collapse. To apply this to Wall Street, unbridled amassing of profit through pure finance with nothing built, no labor, no real service provided, just money chasing money, eventually creates markets that over-react to everything. This sucks wealth out of the real part of the economy especially when massive corrections and crashes hit the markets. Obviously, wealth provides immunity from poverty just as the human immune system guards against disease. However, both can only be maintained and strengthened holistically and ethically, not merely at the speed of computing.

It seems anathema to our belief in and reverence for higher education that PhDs might be drafted into exploitive frontiers of science and technologies that risk backfiring on the masses whom they are supposed to serve. PCBs, dioxin, glyphosate, mercury and EDA (Ethylenediamine) all lace our soils and waterways with a highly toxic, pathogenic cocktail brought to us by a well educated, trained battalion of chemists and bio-engineers. Such poisons are routinely approved by their trusty highly educated collaborators at the EPA, FDA, DEQ and the like.[2]

The very financial magnitude of Monsanto and Dow Chemical assures a whole bevvy of elected officials will protect them from proper regulation. A slight but growing silver lining is the ingredient labeling and warning labeling which much of the food and consumer goods industries have adopted. But exactly why the perpetrators "walk" from their crimes has yet to become a priority for the agencies created to act in the public interest.

One of the farthest reaches of dangerous exploration in algorithms is the field of mass video surveillance. Wire tapping, meta data collecting, contextual speech analysis are not enough for the security state. What we see now are video capture systems deployed in cities that recognize faces, can help with racial profiling and identify a person by their gait or the unique way in which they walk. Talk about big brother, twisted sister and funny uncle.

In "In the Age of the Smart Machine," Shoshona Zuboff looks at ways in which disciplinary technologies have entered the workplace. In the book she cites numerous manufacturing plants that implement a sophisticated system that tracks the progress of their employees, where every keystroke and action is logged. This allows for comprehensive tracking of the procedures of a plant, even afterhours when only one or two workers are onsite and none of the plant managers are present. They are able to access the data remotely, and that data is stored in an electronic archive. The overview system allows the managers to track their employees' behavior and problem solving skills to build an objective picture of the goings-on of the plant. One of the managers she interviewed said, "This computer is like X-ray vision. It makes the people who operate the process very unfriendly or perhaps robotic in an attempt to mimic their captive environment."[3]

A recent online investment newsletter popped out at me with the expression "collaborative robots." What is more, it touted that very futurist threat as an 64 billion dollar industry by 2020.[4] Such a far cry from, "hey Siri, where's a good place for Sushi in Sioux City." Another future problem is the result of Moore's Law: the power of computing has been doubling roughly every 18 months.[5] While the pace of Moore's law may be arguably slowing down, the bad news is computer programmers lag behind a crucial awareness of how accelerating power impacts programming itself. It can be similarly argued that programmers without question, are truly out of touch with the decisions that "runaway algorithms" are capable of making thereby making them a danger to society.

Fire is fire, it either burns or goes out. But water is entirely different in nature when moving or still. A peaceful pond exudes serenity and support of life. It reflects the beauty of the sky and echoes the cry of the loon. But a category five white water rapids in spring will overcome anything that enters its waters. Complete and full compliance to its power may bode deliverance or doom. Nevertheless, the driving force of the rapids is considered in physics, a "weak force," a manifestation of gravity.

The fatal flaw in artificial intelligence and algorithms emerges from the organic complexity of nature itself; and I dare say, of human nature. The beauty of intelligence is our adaptability to the moment and our ability to think retrospectively, peripherally and linearly, simultaneously in real time while performing a task or solving a problem. You want an experienced naturalist to enter the white water, not an autonomous drone.

Undaunted by the fatal flaws of AI, figures like Michael Hayden, erstwhile head of the CIA and NSA want all of our phone calls and emails stored and potentially examined algorithmically for signs of terroristic or other un-American tendencies. To accomplish that, he glibly sought out allies in government who would construct an exculpatory legal defense for the gutting of FISA laws and abandoning of a number of constitutional guarantees.

A human's integration into the natural world is by definition antithetical to artificial intelligence. Ideas and quasi thought generated in the AI world move in a closed, multi-parallel-linear system. Nonlinear or chaotic phenomena are still processed linearly in computers resulting in potentially disastrous outcomes. The decision to launch a missile attack might make perfect sense to a computer based on the conditions and parameters of the moment. But it takes a human being to say no to war.

Justin Rosenstein is a thirty-something tech executive who was the Facebook engineer who invented the "like" button. Now the embodiment of inventor's remorse, he refers in a desultory manner to "bright dings of pseudo-pleasure" as he now carries a cell phone with no app capability and parental controls that keep eyeball substance abuse in check.

"It is very common," Rosenstein says, "for humans to develop things with the best of intentions and for them to have unintended, negative consequences."[6]

Media impressions and clicks are the new universal units of demographic measurement that form the foundations of whole mega industries which daily vanquish the fading entrepreneurs in the heart of our little and not so little towns. To think that we may all be outlived by our algorithmic marketing profiles even sucks all the humor out of my own jaded carapace.

Tristan Harris, a major beneficiary of as well as creator of super algorithms in silicon valley, warns us that a handful of tech companies control billions of minds every day. At a 2017 TED talk he warns,

"I want you to imagine walking into a control room with a bunch of people hunched over a desk with little dials... and that control room will shape the thoughts and feelings of a billion people. This might sound like science fiction, but this happens actually today...I used to be in one of these control rooms."[7]

The ultimate consumerism is the consumption of the human conscience by algorithmically driven machines which know our whereabouts, our purchases, our travels, our net worth, our family configurations, our place on the gender continuum, our nutritional intake and perhaps even our preference for a particular scent in our soap.

In a technofascist world the consumer is ultimately the consumed.

5

HIPPOCRAT OR HYPOCRITE?

Corona versus Coronation

I t is not the exclusive province of Chief Seattle to remind us that all that exists for the common good like air and water is not for sale. None other than Jonas Salk who, had he gotten a plug nickel for every polio case prevented, could have joined the "Fortune five hundred," refused to accept royalties for his vaccine. World health is simply too important to be made scarce by profiteering. Other immunizations and treatments that have come along have ended up enriching the big pharmaceutical labs that developed them as intellectual properties. And the fact that much of the basic research is bankrolled by foundations and academe fails to chasten the venal monopolists out there who hesitate to address a topic that may implicate fearless healers among us in less than perfect practices and outcomes. But I am in good company in the use of the dichotomous title for this chapter, not only because it resembles the title of an episode of a British TV series that has gone around the world, but that it attempts to tell it like it is.

The covid pandemic has brought the world to an "O.K. Corral" style shoot out between those who want the human race to rise to the highest level of cooperation and expertise sharing and those who want to take yet another catastrophe as central casting for the worse actors to make two killings: one in the pharmaceutical market and the other in sheer body count as governments pivot their priorities from human health to market recovery in real time as the virus spreads over the land. Time and time again we see political and corporate entities sink to a state of inverted synergy where the sum of institutional evil is greater than the sum of individual evil of their members. What this means in human terms is that perfectly ethical medical researchers are brought into league with the mavens of intellectual property and proprietary innovation leading to delays in addressing all classes and all peoples globally according to their medical needs to the service of controlling markets and creating scarcities. I know it's hard to believe that whole careers which began in the best of medical schools replete with medical ethics courses and quotes of Hippocrates chiseled in stone over doorways, are dropped into a the mosh pit of profitability while the *Tower of Power* wails on.

All healing arts invite controversy. The belief system between doctor and patient is alchemical as well as biochemical, psychological as well as pharmacological. Even self-love and humor have been known to work wonders in the recuperative process. I grew up with Norman Cousin's "Anatomy of an Illness" in which watching funny movies becomes part of the cure for a neurological disorder. But aside from the matter of how delicate or imperfect the doctor-patient relationship, and the attitude of the patient, the role of modern institutions can bring in issues of institutional malpractice with alarming ramifications.

Medical technology is the area of inquiry in this book that has directly touched more lives-saving some- than any other. But just how the hi tech industry has managed to inveigle a huge profit center for itself that seems never to be supplanted by permanent cures or true progress in medical research reminds one of the permanent war economy where a "go find a war" mentality has set in. Really, how does one avoid conflict of interest in appropriating billions for cancer research leading to a super industry whose goal it is to find the cure that will lead to shutting down the industry itself? Remember, psychologists starve in a sane world.

It is not the purpose of this discourse to criticize established medical practices by pointing out alternatives; there are libraries of books on the subject. We begin rather with the question, why does health care in America average more than $2,000 per individual more than the next highest spender, Switzerland?[1] And may we consider that the whole medical delivery establishment, doctors, hospitals, research and pharma reflect a predatory level of exploitation? If not, then our government would not have created embargos on affordable foreign sourced drugs; nor would oncologists receive direct profits from the prescription of astronomically priced chemotherapy courses;[2] nor would HMO CEOs be paid tens of millions in basic compensation; nor would an appendectomy cost nearly $14,000 in America versus 6-7K in New Zealand.[3]

And while we are at it, why is there a vicious slander campaign against "Medicare for All" or single payer programs couched in red bating terminology? Are lobbyists for big pharma and medical technology behind such a dark PR campaign? One may easily widen the technofascist tent to accommodate all of the above. The brutal reign of predatory capitalists in the health of our country seems to have defeated all levelheaded opposition. The faith all of us put into the Affordable Care Act, that the industry would somehow increase accessibility and affordability, while experiencing a measured level of success in areas of coverage, is now easy prey in a Republican administration- with neo-liberals waiting in the wings. Let's face it the free enterprise has gone out of our health care system, along with, the alleged socialism.

Consider this headline from Ars Technica:

Pfizer CEO Gets 61% Pay Raise – to $27.9 Million – as Drug Prices Continue to Climb. In a recent three-week span, the company hiked 116 drug prices as much as 9.46 percent.[4]

Corporate holders of medical patents are nothing but monopolists. A company like Merck, Pfizer or Johnson and Johnson corners the market on a critical drug and the price goes through the roof. Meanwhile, federal agencies terrorize- less so recently- cannabis growers whose products are proven many times over to provide palliative and curative benefits, yet who have to live with a "schedule one" controlled substance label by the DEA. This same DEA righteously claims that medical marijuana has no accepted medical use; not only tendentious reporting but declaration of war on a vast outlaw subculture of this exponentially growing industry and patient network.

Given the prevalence of the spirit of caring and curing held among physicians in our culture as in the world over, it is particularly dissonant for technology to have intervened in almost every phase of doctor patient and nurse patient contact. Like an unwelcome participant in the intimate setting of a doctor's office. The HMO clinics put doctors on the clock featuring a quota of patients that will be processed hour-by-hour, minute by minute as dictated by the bottom line. Traditional healer-patient eye contact has been replaced by data collection on hand held digital devices and desk tops in the service of voracious informatics. In hospital settings, many institutions have adopted the team approach with specialists being directed like traffic at the intersection where the patient lies helplessly as if waiting for a light that may never change.

We live in an age in which medical technology is being exploited to shore up the barriers to alternative cures sourced from ethno-botanical traditions, ayurvedic practices, traditional Chinese approaches, diet based approaches and others all of which deserve population studies compared side by side with chemo therapies, radiation and surgery. Natural cures will always rise in a society in which prevention and non-proprietary cures are readily available and act as "first responders" to many conditions.

6

THE COUP, THE WHOLE COUP AND NOTHING BUT THE COUP

"I have built my organization on fear"
–Al Capone

Al Capone got it right when he said in effect that the system of laws and regulations proffered exactly what he needed to systematize the practices of graft, bribery, larceny, blackmail, lethal enforcement and all routine business dealings that empowered his enterprises. Laws were simply the scaffolding that enabled him and his associates on both sides of the law to build a stunning high rise. So for every Capone, there is a group of corrupt, venal collaborators on the other side of the desk, the badge or the cash register. The Capone analogy would be a bit far fetched in the context of our tri-cameral government were it not that moon shine has been replaced by fossil fuel, big pharma, GMOs intellectual property rights with profits attached to almost everything we buy and an army of lobbyists who become the "enforcers," in bed with alleged "law makers" practicing all of the derelictions referenced above. What a coup!

In the governing of a state, there are three types of coup:

1. The military coup

2. The soft coup

3. The stealth coup

Few would have an inkling that type one was ever attempted in the U.S.…and they'd be wrong! Do a multi-sourced Google search on General Smedley Butler, Prescott Bush, The Harrimans and you will find that there was a military coup that was waiting in the wings to take down FDR as he was offering the New Deal to America to remedy the Depression.[1]

Conversely, when you replace a bungling, blustering aspiring dictator with a truly professional, credible version of the same thing ideologically then what we have is "the mistake after the mistake," a principle that applies to all of the crime-cover up capers that have back fired including Watergate and Iran Contra. So too it would be wise to remain vigilant about the importing of a "color revolution" as conducted in Ukraine, a neo-liberal specialty traceable to both the Clinton and Obama administrations.[2]

Regime change, a neo-con game plan as well, relies on more aggressive paths to success such as, no-fly zones, drone attacks and Special Forces hits.

But now we get to the real meat of our discourse on technofascism: the taking over of governments and its agencies from within; from within I mean the security state, the military industrial complex along with the drastic manipulation of all levels of political organizations, the majority of elected officials and the "reality making" major media. Welcome to the world of the stealth coup.

Every one of these methods though never called out sufficiently by the sedated press was at play and in place surrounding the Bush 43 victory in 2000. But we are getting ahead of the time line. Those readers who are the "lone gunman" advocates in cases of the assassinations of Lincoln, JFK, MLK, RFK, may want to skip this chapter. And those who feel the Bush 41, 43 (twice) and Trump victories were won fair and square may consider the same. In the case of the democrats, the defeat of Bernie Sanders in the primaries is a perfect fit for the description of a stealth political coup.[3]

Rather than dwelling on lists, by looking a bit deeper at one of the coups we might acquire insights toward researching and analyzing others. When GW Bush declared the 9/11 attacks to be an act of war, not a crime, he set in motion all of the extraordinary powers the executive arrogates to itself in the form of a military monopolization of the national discretionary spending budget, the foreign relations priorities, homeland security apparatus, civil freedom curtailments as well as raising the likelihood of his re-election.

Can this windfall of powers possibly be fortuitous? Regardless of who called in the attacks; despite our response being inadequate in the moment, W was enabled to enact a lockdown on our social freedoms, our economic priorities, and our political diversity. At the same time he was able to increase his popularity as president at a time when it was plummeting in all surveys and polls. This has all of the earmarks of a stealth coup with the same president in office but new actors taking over the reins of government.

When it comes to the spectacle of war, the major media are all over it, duped and distracted – and intimidated into abandoning their role as government critics in residence.

What has ensued is the longest period of continuous military engagement of the United States in history; engagement in numerous countries simultaneously with no end in sight. So the permanent war "economy" so feared by Eisenhower's generation is now escalated to permanent war itself- so much for the relevance of participatory democracy in U.S. governance. The Patriot Act puts wide swathes of the constitution on ice.

What often happens in a democracy is that powerful business interests create what is essentially an election proof hold on their power and wealth. This takes the form of supporting both sides of a two party race. There are instances of giant corporations or whole industries through their PR entities – like the American Dairy Association – making sure that they have a fiscal presence with all major candidates for office. Relying on a spectacle distracted media, few investigative stories ever emerge on this epidemic of corruption. As a lobbyist, once you get past an election you hold your power in the form of pay to play payback. When the next election rolls around the cycle begins again. Now we are approaching the classical definition of fascism itself. By just adding in the imperialist, neo- liberal worldwide exploitive attributes in the way multi-national corporations conduct business to the already existing use of hard power via military might, you have the formula for Mussolini's fondest dream.

Moreover, when the presidency shifts from one party to another and so little change or reform occurs, what are we supposed to conclude? The streets echo with "money out of politics" rewarded by little media resonance in the mainstream. Meanwhile, the election-proof Wall Street-D.C.-backed think tanks and elements within the C.I.A. are designing nefarious "social coups" of their own like the controlling of rock counterculture a generation ago. [4]

One might plausibly suspect that the denial of John Lennon's visa in 1972 based on a very minor marijuana charge, at a time when his radical political star was on the rise might be coincidence. That the rather paranoid Nixon White House was directing efforts against Lennon will remain conjecture without a deep whistle blower. However, in 1980, when I happened to be in San Francisco on business, news of Lennon's murder struck like a tsunami to the town. This, at a time when he had radicalized a generation of young Americans toward peace. And while we are at it, what happened to political rock activism in the latter Viet Nam war years, leaving us with "vanilla" soft rock and antiseptic disco? That the courts had successfully vacated John Lennon's deportation deepens the suspicion that he was on a C.I.A. enemies list at a time when popular support for the war was collapsing.

Some aware journalists mumbled about a soft coup in the White House evidenced by the sheer number of generals situated around the table from day one of the Trump presidency. The coup label is also well earned by what goes on behind the scenes in intra-party politics. It is long passed time to stop blaming the coup of the DNC by the Hillary Machine on Bernie for "not being a real Democrat." Trump is certainly not real anything! Included in the analysis of Bernie is having done more for the Democratic party than they ever did for him. What is far more significant in the role of our venerable parties in electoral politics is that, as long as any individual politician can be bought and owned by fat cat patrons, e.g., Koch brothers and the Mercers, with impunity in both parties, those of us who refuse to countenance such a system may want to consider the following hash tag: #beyondparty.

Little wonder the coup has come home to roost in the country which has aided and abetted coups around the world from Iran to Honduras to Haiti to Chile to Hawaii to name a few. So too, the fingers now pointing abroad to election meddling should be pointed inward, a theme I shall return to frequently in this descant.

The sale of $400 billion –that's billion with a "b"- in armaments to the Saudis in Donald Trumps first year in office, not only gave a deadly boost to US trade, but it allowed the Saudis to essentially buy their security by enriching our leading export industry and give fresh voice to the sad role we play in continued bloodshed in the middle east.

Eye Contact

Ideas were nowhere to be seen in the beginning
the big bang came and went without fanfare
planets clung to their appointed orbits
comets flirted with galaxies

the grand evolution stuck in its interminable rut .
words arose from somewhere
words and ideas long after the fact
whole landscapes of words
spewed from the twitching mouth of literacy

stories of determinacy and destiny poured forth
the supernatural meaning of it all
stars in lock step with souls
the white noise of purpose

eye contact is the one exception
waiting for the thought reluctant to attend
eyes locked when we are about
to say nothing.

7

Technofoodist Takeover

"Let food be thy medicine and medicine be thy food"
– Hippocrates

How many more eons are we to be inundated by processed foods pumping us full of high fructose corn syrup, carrageenan, sodium nitrate, hydrogenated oil, BHA preservative and Aspartame to name a few? The wholly bought and paid for junk science that supports this abysmal diet- as ruthless on the environment as on our bodies- is conducted on revered campuses across the country and serves as witness to a misapplication of lab technology to the service of the technofascist agenda. At the same time, the most disproportionately affected segment of society, those who can't afford to shop organic or cook-fresh are the legacy poor and working poor. Co-opting science itself in the bargain, to the service of an aggressive business plan only further proves the point.

One concerted reaction to the onslaught of biotechnology in foods however, which is gradually and incrementally correcting the situation – though not nearly fast enough in ridding ourselves of GMOs, glyphosate, Malathion and other organophosphates - is the proliferating organic food industry and anti GMO movement. [1] We can begin to experience the extent of the problem by walking into our local hardware store, super market, builder and garden supply and taking a deep breath. The preponderance of weed preventive grass seed, insecticides et al is overwhelming. And to think that employees have to breathe that stuff every day. How is this related to food?

If it were up to Monsanto almost no seed would go into the ground without being "Roundup ready" which is to say laced with insecticide to kill or inhibit pests that reduce the crop yield. Of course they may also contain toxins that reduce longevity and health in the humans who ingest them. They also leech nasty chemicals into the environment which work their way into the water table and many of our creeks and rivers. Genetically modified seeds, especially corn, developed to increase yield, attack the human immune system and are known to engender allergies, especially respiratory conditions in children. [2] The fact that genetic patents assign intellectual property rights to their developers means sales of the seeds originates from a single source and all profits from those sales accrue to that source which in turn means that farmers become captive customers of Monsanto. A true progressive argument against this would be that you cannot patent nature. The neo-liberal position is: "let's feed the world"…. but first, reap the profits.

The flagrant commodification of natural plants by patent seeking corporations like W.R. Grace and Monsanto plays a key role in international agreements like GATT- General Agreement of Trade and Tariffs- and Tripp-Trade Related Intellectual Property [3]. The effect these predatory entities and legal rip offs have on traditional and aboriginal farming and food gathering is devastating in that communities of growers are forced to pay retail for seeds and prohibited by regulators from keeping or developing their own strains. Intellectual property recognition simply installs a technofascist approach in agribusiness wherein society and its natural diversity is redefined as patent violation or its equivalent depending on the legal lingo of the country in which it occurs.

As we careen toward the climate tipping point and ask what we as individuals can do for eco-sustainability, one surprising response might be "don't go out for that hamburger!."

Climate experts tell us that methane is a far more potent green house gas than CO_2. About 25% of methane emissions in the U.S. are produced in the digestive process of farm animals principally bovine but also by sheep and to a lesser extent all of the other farm animals. At the same time farmed meat is a water guzzler with one 1/3-pound burger requiring 660 gallons of water. To put this in perspective, an orange represents a water investment of 13 gallons.[4]

When it gets to what is affectionately referred to as "externalities," that is the secondary effects of human activity e.g. the fouling of an aquifer by fracking operations, the livestock sector is one of the greatest producers of CO_2 and nitrous oxide in addition to the methane already spoken of. Most dramatic and egregious of all may be the rapid destruction of the Amazon rain forest by clear cutting, burning and conversion to grazing land for … guess what … that hamburger I disabused you of.

Hence it is now impossible to be a one-issue activist. Aboriginal rights are land rights, are environmental rights, are fishing rights, and are civil rights. What is best for our native brothers and sisters is best for all of us. I repeat, all of us.

Don't have a food fight with bacon lovers or flan fanatics. If you wish to reduce your carbon and your environmental stress footprint in general you know what to do, without counseling and especially without those much vaunted "conversations" everyone is having at the edge of the precipice.

Technofascism loves the corporatization, deregulation and capitalist exploitation of a commodity known as food. Growing a head of lettuce in the ground doesn't do it for the corporatists. We in fact see the super market model as the major retail delivery system for foods and household items which virtually guarantees the crisis of high carbon refrigeration and transportation, over-packaging, flagrant use of chemicals, and shirking good nutritional standards for profit and more profit.

We can explain the enormous environmental impact of a small package of frozen peas to a fourth grader. The pea is picked and thrown in a bin with a million more that are trucked a distance to a regional processing plant –with energy guzzling machinery. Sorting and ranking take place, packaging is fashioned from trees and chemicals, ink, design staff. The completed packages are frozen, sent to a distribution warehouse, loaded on to refrigerated trucks which in turn make a stack-train car voyage to a super market refrigerated unloading dock, then trucked again to a refrigerated warehouse, then again to the super market where they begin their refrigerated shelf life of a month or two in the frozen food case at the market. So by the time one pea roles off the fork into the reluctant mouth of our fourth grader, it represents the carbon production of a giant beach ball filled with CO_2.

"Buy local" practices in foods are slowly catching on in a minority- mind you- of the population. Yet it is no accident that Walmart is now shrewdly the biggest purveyor of organic foods in the country . Sustainable products and practices that fortuitously generate corporate profits are a windfall benefit somewhat devoid of altruism. Nevertheless, these practices need to be encouraged by those at the forefront of climate and health activism as a step in the right direction.

Then why do most medical doctors fall silent around nutritionally based healing practices? Ever heard of anti-carcinogenic foods? What about antioxidant rich vegetables and roots? Are doctors enamored of the profits in pharmaceuticals and surgery over ways to avoid them in the first place?

As far back as the Greeks and Romans, food was categorized by its medicinal value. Honey was classically considered a medicine as was wine; hardly refutable today by experts in metabolism.

The one element without which there would be no food as we know it is water. The corporate privatization of water as a human resource by entities like Nestle and Coca Cola is nothing short of abundant resource theft and scarcification.[5]

The preeminent radical thinker and scientist Vandana Shiva has written:

"Global corporations are taking advantage of the demand for clean water, a demand which resulted from environmental pollution. Even though the corporations tap clean water resources in non-industrialized, unpolluted regions, they refer to their bottling practice as 'manufacture' of water … bottled water production is expected to double every two years."[6]

Perhaps this brings us far afield from our book's title and theme. Or does it? We are simply looking at a complex system. If for example we were looking at proliferation and progressive increase of wild fires in the western U.S. and failed to factor in global warming, growing drought and other consequences of human activity, the trail of evidence would grow cold indeed. Our aquifers are ailing thanks to so-called modern farming practices. Contamination begins in the board rooms of the usual suspects: Dow, Bayer, Scotts, Ortho and Monsanto. Industrial farmers are slowly waking up to the realization that they are being put in the pipeline of the chemical factory to dinner table business with no way out save an ag-revolution.

Between the global practice of converting native flora into grazing land for farm animals and the genetic distortion of seeds we encounter synergistic forces of environmental collapse neck and neck headed toward the finish line.

There is a racial element to the full cybernetic mercenary approach to food production as well. Minorities are disproportionately seeking good jobs as the way out of chronic poverty out of fear of being ground down by white privilege into a wretched existence. By buying into the high tech world might they be tempted to self ethnic cleanse, turning away from their own culture? Technofascism frowns on heritage. Rudolph Steiner, German educator and mystic, said it well when he warned that science changed the nature of work in that the true identity of the worker, their humanity and culture, essentially disappeared into their job in science or technology.[6]

8

"For Sale By Owner"
on the White House Lawn

"Humans merely share the Earth. We can only protect the land, not own it."
                                                    – Chief Seattle

W
e have been taught that the White House, built by slaves, was a national monument as well as a domicile for the present POTUS. But little did we know that this trophy piece of real estate along with its occupants could be "purchased" on the market for measly millions. Turning our attention briefly to the Clintons, not long after leaving the White House their net worth increased mysteriously by millions.[1] In addition to their head of state status, they had also used the Clinton Foundation to accept indirect gifts principally to broker influence with their donors in the form of access to the President, staff and members of congress, a venal behavior. Donald Trump pulls it off in a slightly different way by using the presidency itself to build his brand, making sure it impacts all future Trump enterprises while in or out of the White House: this, in violation of the emollients clause of the constitution. On the global trade industrial map Washington D.C. is just one pushpin. The Clintons and the Trumps work the full 360 degrees, ten more then the 350 ppm of the safe level of CO_2. So in a technofascist world, rule by tommy gun is elevated to labyrinthine investment accounts, in turn masked behind shell corporations and dark offshore banks.[2]

Multinational corporations have little regard for borders. When the labor movement appeals to congress a few good listeners may be found only to be summarily nullified by the offshoring practices of uncooperative employers. The message is this: yanking the whole plant can defeat too strong a union.

Keeping a campaign promise by power, control and manipulation are so important to technofascists that they will forego sustainable profits just to keep the under classes in their place, to wit the resistance to vast infrastructure and public works projects that create jobs, new tax payers, new wealth and profits for the private sector as well. Defying the principles of good business because it is too inclusive of people is a form of bigotry in and of itself let alone entitlement. Additionally, as Milton Freedman and Alan Greenspan have descanted, job insecurity is an economic driver of a strong market economy.[3]

As we write, lead is infused in the veins of people in Flint Michigan. And now we learn that circa 2000 U.S. cities are suffering higher levels of lead than Flint.[4] It is wrong to speak of this horrendous act as a mistake or miscalculation. Substandard city services and exposure to health hazards is a subliminal agenda item in technofascism 101. In many cities it is well known that the rich side of town could indeed easily assist the poor side. Congress and the President could also take action but they are too busy making deals instead of conducting government with integrity.

This begs the question, aren't we past the point of going out and winning the next election? Is there a Democrat in office who can address the monolithic wall of resistance of the deep state and the deeper economic cabal? We can't use the Bernie argument…look what happened to him!

To quote myself, "One measure of wealth and power is the number of servants you have. One measure of freedom is the absence of masters."

In the words of Eduardo Galeano, renown Latin American journalist and writer:

"In the United States, the sale of political favors is legal and can be carried on openly- no need to pretend, no risk of scandal. Over ten thousand bribery pros work in Washington, plying their trade with members of Congress and the tenants of the White House"

This is an obvious reference to the K Street gang, otherwise known as lobbyists, referenced here by the author, Galeano in his book, "Upside Down."[5]

Meanwhile, in the "other" wing of the White House, not regaled with a TV series, there dwelt what many think of as the evil genius behind the Bush 43 regime. A man with the initials D.C., fortuitous or not, manifested a virtual board room for Halliburton whose no bid enrichment from our little wars broke every rule for conflict of interest in the book. Some say that the little "sale pending" tag on the White House for sale sign remained for the eight years of "D.C. does D.C.." Oh, to be a political cartoonist so I could create the visual for all this….

And on the other side of the mythical political isle lurks Nancy Pelosi who, while in office, has mushroomed her wealth into the hundred million category. How she is able to call herself the leader of the "people's party" and decry income inequality is the epitome of hypocrisy. No free passes for political hacks.

As a direct beneficiary of massive political donations from the private prison industry, little wonder that the Trump administration was filling beds nation wide with immigrant detainees. Trump did not invent U.S. border policy but stooped to novel extensions of it by separating immigrant children from their detained parents, a heinous injustice under the Universal Declaration of Human Rights and other conventions. Not since Nazi concentration camps have we seen such atrocities committed directly toward children. President Clinton showed regrets, too little too late, for driving the private corrections industry nation wide. It is on his shoulders and Obama's that the Trump administration practiced moral turpitude in the highest.

9

AROUND THE WORLD IN 80 MEGATONS

"Let's make war a controlled substance"

– J.K.

...*"wars, especially in our time, are always wars against children, indeed our children."*
– Howard Zinn

Sure thing, democracy has come to the military. Each general arrayed around the conference table at the Pentagon gets to suggest where the next intervention, invasion, "shock and awe," overt or covert, will occur. Then they vote.

How can one begin to innumerate the brilliant ordinance and ballistic devices combined with the pyramid of legacy armaments that regale our military? There is a piece of hardware for every job, from armor piercing bullets to flash grenades to self-healing body armor. Each stage in the long history of organized military combat acts to heighten the death-to-strike ratio as well as more rapid delivery, more accurate aim, all the way up to epic arsenals of overkill. Here is where technology lowers the cost of fabrication and with that increases accessibility to non-state actors or rogue entities. In other words a very small country could acquire a very big nuclear bomb. There is no greater proof that technology exists without codes of ethics than the gargantuan arsenals of nuclear missiles in silos all over the world whose developers worked on little fragments of the whole like little worker bees not noticing that the hive hangs over the edge of an abyss. This leads to a collective state of pathological absence of conscience providing all but the highest-ranking participants with a kind of deniability of awareness or responsibility for the whole.

Immediately after World War II, the U.S., far and away the leading armaments dealer in the world, felt it had an exclusive on nuclear weapon development. The outlook changed a bit when the USSR detonated an atomic bomb in 1949. The UK then France and China followed shortly. The combined firepower of this quintet if released in a global war would amount to population overkill with a multi-year nuclear winter to follow.

Just why such a perfect storm did not signal a reversal and build down of this devil's inventory eludes sanity and morality.

It was several years after China joined the nuclear club that the nuclear Nonproliferation Treaty was drafted and signed. The fact that four more nations joined the club after the (NPT) including India, Israel, Pakistan and North Korea, brought the dream of arms reduction into slow motion at best, and a feeling of futility at worst.[1] What brings the issue of technofascism into the picture is the unmitigated disregard for human life present and future through involvement in what is essentially a global extinction consortium of nations.

American presidents, both Republican and Democrat, have supported the defense industries that supply an astronomically exorbitant catalogue of products and services for the efficient conduct of wars. The killing of peace itself, a modus operandi of hegemonic statecraft, is a seminal element in the etiology of technofascism. It is the utter disregard for the immense harm a technology presents to society that fuses it to economic practices and beliefs. The economy of armaments is the economy of oppression.

So mystified toward war and global political chaos is the pentagon, as promoted by the American propaganda apparatus, that all outside efforts at apprehending the criminal minds to subject them to international protocols and regulations are thwarted by our government itself.

A lesser-known policy of the American military elites is the concept of "full spectrum domination." I believe I heard this first from a defense analyst. The Air Force is in the lead on this and can certainly look at the world as full battlefield map with ability to deploy anywhere within hours or strike ballistically within minutes. Green lighting such disgustingly aggressive policies brings in several administrations Democratic and Republican. So it goes with peace plans.

One enduring goal of technofacisism is to liberate science, technology and business from moral circumspection. All evidence of this trend lies in the objects lying around, the weapons, the white elephant interceptor jets in an empty sky, the incongruous grid iron aircraft carriers bobbing in desolate oceans, the paramilitary flack-jacketed police lining the parade routes of pacifist marches.

All the while, surreal maps of the world exist with each U.S. military installation indicated by a dot. True, some are actually populated by actual troops, others may be for drones or logistics; but the sum total has hovered around 800 worldwide since the Bush 43 administration.[1] The expense for this mega-maniacal enterprise would pay for America's health care and college tuition several times over. So much for our "beacon to the world" status in the twenty first century.

No greater collusion between advanced scientific research and real world outcomes has been more epic than the development of nuclear energy en route to the bomb. Einstein himself reluctantly brought the feasibility of atomic weapons closer to Harry Truman under the duress of the Nazis and WW II; an act he was to deeply regret for the rest of his life. One Einstein quote says it all:

"The unleashed power of the atom has changed everything save our modes of thinking, and thus we drift toward unparalleled catastrophe."[2]

And from acclaimed journalist John Pilger:

"It is not news that the safeguards on our nuclear weapons have been quietly removed and that the United States is now spending $46 million per hour on nuclear weapons: that's $46 million every hour, 24 hours a day, every day."[3]

DOOMSDAY

Doomsday
was Wednesday
surprising everyone,
who had planned
their Thursdays
from dawn to setting sun

who had planted vernal bulbs
now and then along the lane
who had smartly smiled
at the news forecasting rain,

it surprised the village mayor
who planned to run again

but alas, doomsday
was Wednesday
lest we pretend
doomsday was Wednesday

Wednesday was the end.

10

ASSANGE AND MANNING AS HERALD ANGELS

"Truth is a state secret"

– J.K.

The American people are not all couch potatoes. They are not all seated in rank and file in front of screens all hours of the day eager to be fed the scripted tabloid virtual reality beamed at them by a consortium of corporate media ink toners in collaboration with deep state psycho-babel scripters. That said, our captains of communication have failed to perceive that a vast majority of the population possess perfectly fine bullshit detectors and may be fooled only "some of the time."

The masses are also increasingly open to alternative news sources that are not corporate shills and who tend to speak truth to power.

Sorry you Wikileaks detractors, the jig is up. Faux fact checkers and authenticity narcs trying to discredit and demonize courageous whistle blowers are wearing out their credibility. It would be nice if the UK wore out the "wanted for questioning" or "fleeing a warrant" canard against Julian. But to be held for publishing the unvarnished truth reconfirms one's un-impeachability, albeit imminent danger to the established order plain and simple.

Once Sweden dropped their delusional non-charges, one would think that freedom was imminent for Assange. But, for the UK authorities to be dragging their feet on even saving face for their lock-step complicity with the U.S.' absolute fixation on charging him with espionage is ludicrous and of course, remains perilous for the victim. Julian Assange is a powerful threat to the technofascist's obsession with controlling the carpet messaging of the alternate version of reality they "script."

Developing hack-proof encryption has been very hard for those plying the left shoulder of the information highway. Meanwhile there has been precedent for CIA interfering directly in Ecuadorian elections, a nefarious practice that was surely rolled out to no avail in 2017, as Correa's last term of office came to a conclusion.[1]

The ultimate goal of Wikileaks is primary source journalism which should make the world ultimately safer for free societies as well as for commerce. But a free society is the enemy of the corporate state. The wide swath of jungle and earth and ocean and teeming masses qua eco-insurgents that the exploiters victimize, drives their victims into ever desperate measures to the point where they can be driven into appearing to be "the bad guys" as pusillanimously labeled by a succession of American presidents.

"Collateral Murder," released by Wikileaks via Chelsea Manning in 2010 is not a long, clear, broadcast quality video yet it incandescently exposes the fictive narrative of American military presence in the Middle East. What are the caged journalists going to do now post Collateral Murder once they realize their employers are wholly owned subsidiaries of the security state and are beholden to the business of military propaganda making? The fact that Reuters crew were victims of the attack should, in a just world, radicalize Reuters forever. Stay tuned ... [2]

A likely explanation for the rampant obsession of the major media over alleged Russian interference in the 2016 presidential election is that we are systematically being thrown off the trail of the misdeeds of the DNC vis a vis Bernie as revealed by leaked emails published by Wikileaks.

We are being mired as well in a diversion that impedes the process of looking at our electoral system as a whole, complete with gerrymandering, buying elections, super delegates, dark money et al. The cold war maintained a binary equilibrium of instability which can be thought of as the basis for the military profit center. Naturally there are those who yearn to bring that all back and appear to be on the ascendant.

You know you live in a dystopia when the greatest contributors to transparency and accountability in government are held in detention while the biggest of the crooks stare out of their high rises at skylines of limitless loot. We live in a time when a Presidential fact finding committee equals cover up and a congressional committee hearing equals smear.

When Chelsea Manning was stripped of her Harvard Visiting Fellow status, society was handed on a silver platter in plain view for all to see, a flagrant admission that anyone or any organization that opposes technofascist practices in our government must be impeached, besmirched, incarcerated, tortured as prelude to being run out of town. The data of the imaging system alone on Apache attack helicopters, once fed onto computer screens, then interpreted as target data for remote video game trained gunners, potentially results in a donnybrook of deadly force unleashed against the largely innocent and is taken as a technofascist trophy; one that several presidents and their defense departments have relied on in the global war against terrorism. Never mind that 9/11 was declared an act of war rather than crime scene even before the site stopped smoldering, though as it turns out Bin Laden, the "mastermind" of it all, was likely receiving dialysis in a Pakistani hospital. For those who refute such a likelihood we do have on the record from President Bush 43 himself that "The idea of focusing on one person really indicates to me people don't understand the scope of the mission. Terror is bigger than one person. He's just a person who's been marginalized."[3]

That is why, as Harvard alum, I am faced with living through what I dolefully refer to as "the first extinction of VERITAS."

Below is the text of a letter to the editor or Harvard Magazine I submitted on hearing that Manning had been dis-invited from a Harvard guest fellows residency in fall 2017:

CHELSEA MANNING IN THE YARD to Harvard Magazine

I have been looking everywhere for alternate definitions of the Latin wor, *veritas*. Having learned of the long collaborative relationship between Harvard and the CIA, nowhere can I find room for secondary meanings like disinformation, regime change, proxy wars or assassinations in that definition.

So now the CIA has done all of us a big favor by "coming out" in plain sight –albeit in the dark of night- as a security agency that leans heavily on its academic partners to polish its image as a paragon federal agency in our country and the world. All this despite its role as covert violent disrupter of the political life of sovereign nations, concurrent with instigation of regime change and bloody anti-democratic upheaval the world over. This schema often referred to as full spectrum dominance is the most anti-democratic and anti-humanitarian diplomatic principle a nation can pursue. It also shakes to the very core the nature of higher education as sanctuary and beacon of academic freedom and incorruptible intellectual integrity.

Harvard, ever the CIA acolyte, appears to have stood up and been counted by the bullying of Chelsea Manning in its school yard. In so doing, Harvard has simultaneously stood against its core maxim of "veritas" which is burned into the school's coat of arms while helping to invalidate the only power the people have against the secrecy and perfidy of our police state: whistle blowing. Who is the keeper of veritas? Is it the CIA or Manning? And who is the enemy of veritas?

One could say that this was a defining moment at Harvard, were it not that this "moment" is nothing new. Ultimately, an academic institution must embody its legacy as reflected in its students, faculty and the finest traditions of academic freedom, not the covert interests of the state.[5]

Joel Kabakov PhD GSAS '77

For the CIA as a powerful covert organ of the state to lose its commanding sway over the great American audience- as it is unfortunately seen- by not being able to own the message being framed and transmitted over the major media, is unacceptable. Unrepentant punks –as the media cast them- like Snowden, Manning, Assange and Drake loom as a menace as they grow in popularity to near legendary heights and simply must be reined in, if not figuratively lynched or physically incarcerated as so many escaped slaves from the information plantation.

The success of alternative media can be measured by the magnitude of the campaign against it. A truly robust democracy can certainly withstand foreign news and commentary sources like Al Jazeera, RT –now being asked to register as a "foreign agent"- and Wikileaks.org.[4]

While the growing list of investigative information sources largely survives, we need to remain vigilant in opposing efforts to attack them in the corporate, government sponsored media as well as the halls of congress. Accusations of propaganda in alternative media are cognitive inversions to say the least.

So too, our population has been saturated by salvo after salvo of opinion polls. What appears as a perfectly innocent polling question on politics for example is actually a meticulously crafted leading question that "pushes" a certain response such as "if North Korea refuses to cease development of nuclear weapons does the U.S. have the obligation to intervene with military force?" What is not provided is the prefatory remark that around a dozen nations have developed weapons of just that description and that a couple of the above refuse to sign any non-proliferation treaty, and as if that weren't enough, North Korea has shown willingness to discuss a "freeze for a freeze" where sanctions would be lifted in exchange for placing their nuclear program on hold. Hence, what is omitted from the question completely controls the outcome of the poll and creates a false impression that the people are in lock step agreement with the generals.

The American corporate news media, print and pixel, are under the impression that what does not survive the twenty-four hour news cycle ceases to exist. What is more, those whose misdeeds are swept up in the media are guaranteed to wane with the new dawn like a kind of induced amnesia. This is what a Donald Trump relied upon in making some of his wilder and preposterous claims and insults. Launch a war on Monday and it sinks below the awareness horizon by Friday.

We are now living through another tantalizing release of JFK assassination documents. Only a fool would not equate the forest of redactions with cover up of the highest order. Pure contempt for transparency or disregard for the right to know of the citizenry is not an adequate explanation for what is going on. We do know that Lyndon Johnson rescinded JFKs planned troop withdrawal from Viet Nam. We also know that JFK was at odds with the CIA on Cuba and on and on…

I wonder what Wikileaks has on this in its mind palace. Authors like Douglass, Russell and Janney are taking matters into their own hands regarding getting to the bottom of an apex moment in American history without which we continue to live a collective lie.[5]

Ground Zero

Here I sit at ground zero
formerly known as a bus stop
waiting for the usual big blue
that takes us to
ground zero
formerly known as the ocean
whose former islands lie beneath the waves

We know there are those
who tried to contain ground zero
way out in an undocumented place
in the desert

Just this once, they said
we'll cut loose a tiny glimpse of hell
at this tiny pin on a map

But that's when ground zero overflowed
it's container
and like a raging river at flood
escaped from high desert to lowlands
country to city
carried on winds and currents
carried in bombs on the bellies of jets
piled on decks of great nuclear carriers
followed by robotic eyes as blips on screens
delivering their deadly pay loads
with every in breath, with every bowl of ionized corn
and bean.

Oh, here comes my bus.

Chapter Eleven

The redundancy of chapter number and title is no coincidence. Banks and finance institutions have been leading the way of late in hatching novel predatory schemes with a full suite of technological tools at the ready. Worth mentioning first is the most recent practice of sub-prime auto loans. In a stable economy there would be fewer brand new cars on the road. The default rate on new car loans at this writing is hovering around 30%. People who are going under just keeping up with their rent, working two or three jobs, paying back mammoth school loans, living on a fixed retirement should not be sweet talked by car dealerships. The Committee for Better Banks reports:

> "A decade after the mortgage crisis financial companies continue to extend risky loans at high interest rates, bundling those loans into securities to sell to eager Wall Street investors, and booking big profits and revenues. This is today's subprime auto lending business and regulators and attorneys general in multiple states are taking note. The industry is worth more than $26 billion and growing fast, and it poses a threat to low-income consumers who need transportation to remain in the labor market. Its aggressive lending and collections practices have the potential to impact the economic well-being of millions of families." [1]

First among subprime auto lenders is Santander Consumer USA, a Dallas-based subsidiary of the Spanish global banking giant Santander Group. Santander has spent the years since the Great Recession purchasing debt in the subprime auto lending market and now controls nearly a third of this lucrative market[2]

Unsolicited credit cards are handed out like candy for similar reasons. Credit reporting agencies practice their own kind of star system where 700 and up are the survivors and all who fall below are losers. It doesn't matter that you have paid your mortgage on time for twenty years. If you make a couple of slow payments or have a financial emergency that maxes out all of your consumer credit you are now sorted and ranked from excellent to good. God forbid you pay cash for everything, have lay-away deals and zero credit card debt for then, you are in the credit basement. Then there are the consolidation companies who bundle all of your debt in marathon pay back schemes which merely relieve your monthly budget a bit in trade for years of obligation. So let me get this straight: those of us who need low cost financing the most are sorted by algorithms into the top interest rates out of which we may never break while the secure and wealthy among us get all of the bargains out there in credit cards, mortgage interest et al. For this we have awesome technology to thank in calculating everyone's spot on the totem pole.

In 2017 Americans were more burdened by student loan debt than ever. You've probably heard the statistics: Americans owe over $1.4 trillion in student loan debt, spread out among about 44 million borrowers. That's about $620 billion more than the total U.S. credit card debt. In fact, the average Class of 2016 graduate has $37,172 in student loan debt, up six percent from the previous year.[3] But how does this break down at a more granular level? Are student loans being used to attend public or private universities? Is it mostly from four-year or graduate degrees? What percentage of overall graduates carry debt? Are more grads utilizing private student loan consolidation and refinancing? Rather than answering point to point the above list of derivative questions, we simply know that all of the above have accumulated enough debt to:

1. forgive with the stroke of a presidential pen

2. forgive by congressional legislation

3. guarantee the continued decline of the middle class

4. jeopardize all U.S. higher education and lose worldwide academic status .

5. increase the authoritarian and oppressive trajectory of government commensurate with the decline of quality education in general.

To reiterate for all Americans, credit ratings have become an accepted way of financial life for hapless consumers. It's as if waking up everyday in a strait jacket makes you grateful for not being a one-armed wall paper hanger. Well, nobody's perfect. What is really going on is that interest rates on consumer debt, mortgages, car loans, credit cards are all indexed to your credit rating; this while we are being told to improve our credit scores just as we slowly sink into the quagmire of "debt lag." The real time fine tuning of credit ratings is technology based. It doesn't matter that you have owned your home for thirty years and have not missed a mortgage payment. You can't refinance at a good interest rate unless you have a slew of credit cards with plenty of head room in their limits. And of course, when all of this forces you into the red, the chapter eleven vultures are there to "rescue" you and open you up to the next cycle of life in the squirrel cage of the credit cartels.

Returning to our chapter title, bankruptcies are an exercise en route to endless debt now that things like student loans and all manner of repayment programs are tacked on to any settlement. It is widely known that at present most bankruptcies are triggered by one serious illness or hospitalization.[4] In short, buyer beware of the dangerous words "you have been approved."

12

OCCUPY THE LANGUAGE

"We don't need a book burning if we smear the authors"

=J.K.

Language is both a verbal and a written conveyer of communication in humans. It is so imprinted into our brain cells and facial anatomy in early childhood that multitudes of foreign speakers living in the U.S. for most or all of their lives, never relinquish their foreign accents. It's as if the only way they could deal with English is to synthesize it with their mother tongue. Even for native born speakers, the continuum of accents coincides roughly with the geographic region of their origin. The Western Virginia accent and inflection is closer to Eastern Kentucky than to Richmond or analogously, Baltimore is in the "Philly"- Southern New Jersey "accent neighborhood." In contrast, true polyglots who master numerous languages with fairly authentic accents are rare indeed.

Propagandists and Public Relations experts know how to command the attention of varied audiences through the manipulation of language. This alone makes foul cause for our government in its infinite war of words in order to exquisitely control messaging in every nuance...including what gets omitted.

"The two sides clashed"...."The demonstrators clashed with police" are perfect ways to reframe the true nature of non-violent protest. When the cops move in, chaos ensues and everyone is perceived to be a combatant, even the ones just rolling into fetal position.

Standing Rock was an exquisitely scripted brutally effective security operation aimed at distorting the true non-violent nature of the water protectors. Were it not for a few brave videographers and reporters, the bad cops would have won the battle both physically and in the theater of public opinion.

Another object of exploitation is the school-of-fish groupthink phenomenon of a somewhat less awake segment of the population.

To have a real school of fish, do you need a teacher/leader?

"It turned out that stickleback fish preferred to follow larger over smaller leaders," said Ashley Ward of Sydney University. "Not only that, but they also preferred fat over thin, healthy over ill, and so on. The part that really caught our eye was that these preferences grew as the group size increased, through some kind of positive social feedback mechanism."

"Their consensus arises through a simple rule," said David Sumpter of Uppsala University. "Some fish spot the best choice early on, although others may make a mistake and go the wrong way. The remaining fish assess how many have gone in particular directions. If the number going in one direction outweighs those going the other way, then the undecided fish follow in the direction of the majority."[1]

No, human society is not just like a school of fish and please don't quote the text above to insist otherwise. However over a vast population pseudo consensus making is a common implement on the tool belt of the PR mavens. Now just substitute the expression, "larger over smaller media footprint" (for larger fish preferred) in following larger over smaller potential leaders. This would also comport with a fabricated diminution of the image of a potential leader by de-emphasizing him/her on the media e.g. Bernie. The definition of the "leader image" would describe the followers as those who relinquish most measures of excellence for the superficial ones ergo, "Abe Lincoln was the tallest" or "JFK was glamorous." Moreover once a plurality falls in line, the whole society suddenly looks conformist. Pictures of Mussolini and Hitler in crowded squares and stadiums are hauntingly referential of the school-of-fish rubric. To round out the picture, Chinese, Russian and U.S. –especially parade images- complete the full political force of mass conformity.

At this writing it would appear that the truth warriors of language; those who realize that the language itself is under hostile occupation are continuing their siege against the propaganda and censoring organs of government and the corporatists with all stops pulled out: this is playing out in the domains of the internet, with leakers and whistle blowers, alternative news sites as well as intrepid teaching and writing in our institutions of higher learning.

The major media treat news consumers as just that: "consumers." The consumer wakes up with a bowl of Captain Crunch and tunes in Fox news, ABC, CNN, you name it; perfect fodder for funneled and tunneled disinformation. Little sanctuary is to be found from the din of tabloid journalism on NPR as substantiated by their anchor sponsors, the Kochs, Walmart, MacDonalds , sponsors that are to be autonomically pleased and certainly not have their toes stepped on.

Now what is to be made of the fact the a media giant itself, Time Warner, manifesting as CNN in news and talk formats turns out to be among the top ten donors to a particular presidential candidate? Some of us are old enough to remember Jefferson Airplane's Grace Slick descanting, "go ask Alice, when she's ten feet tall!" But I say "go ask Hillary."[2] Nevertheless, praise the lord for good radical reportage holding forth across the landscape and webscape of late with sites like "Global Research" from Canada, "Consortium News," and, especially on the environment and racism, "Democracy Now!." None of the above are free of their attachment to the present two party system- an entirely subjective assessment on my part. And they all need to stay in business hence, certain topics like controlled demolition are underreported.

The action-verb equivalent of occupy is to take back. For any showman to be greeted by empty seats in the theater is a career wrecker. For any wild palomino to start a one-horse stampede, regardless of what he tramples in his path is fairly harmless. That's where we come in. The gawkers who show up in the first place; who serve as "viewing audiences" may want to consider staying home, tuning out, not fueling the fire of spectacle. Our minds and hearts cannot be hostilely occupied if we swim contrary to the school of fish.

The deep state relies heavily on the control of language and framing of the thin slice of reality they want us to focus upon. The goal is to never allow the ruling elites to be brought within reach of prosecution. If one person, even a president is scapegoated for all the ills of the system like a big fat proxy, it will never change the system. So root all you want for the demise of Nixon, Bush 43, the Clintons, Obama and Trump. All we will get is a diversionary prosecution followed by business as usual.

There is a new face of tyranny and it has no face. When our every purchase, every email, every affiliation, every trip is captured in a state sponsored data base, we begin to distinguish the vague outlines of institutional tyranny. There are no monuments or statues to the security state but the results of its reign over our lives is just as brutal. Good bye Mussolini, hello NSA, DIA and CIA.

The world of jurisprudence manages to inhabit a somewhat alien world of linguistic expression. The jury of peers, especially in civil cases, maintain a much higher level of candor and originality in their deliberations and verdicts than one might expect. It's as if the prying eyes of the judge and prejudice of society at large has been left on the threshold of the court house.

A major linguistic piracy has taken place in the intersection between racism and law enforcement regarding the bestowal of terrorist status. If the shooter is white, European Caucasian, they are a "disturbed individual" no matter the body count or style of delivery of the deadly attack.

Terrorist status may be earned, on the other hand, by a muslim as if every such act were strictly politically motivated.

There seems to be a low intensity battle royal going on continuously between culture and what I call anti-culture. When you plug into media, you are plugging into endless artificial scripts despite the warmth and apparent sincerity of the speaker. Media personalities have surrendered their true feelings, personalities and natal culture. In a way this is the final frontier of linguistic occupation because it takes the whole being with it, leaving an empty surname and a live microphone on the altar of virtual existence.

Strolling through a check out counter at the super market today I glimpsed the cover of Rupert Murdoch's recently acquired National Geographic magazine. Guess what three countries are the "happiest on earth." Well, Cost Rica is no surprise. But Singapore?

One example of their generous attitude toward capital punishment:

> A mandatory death penalty is passed for individuals convicted of trafficking in:
> -15 grams or more of heroin
> -30 grams or more of cocaine
> -200 grams or more of hashish
> -500 grams or more of cannabis
> -1200 grams or more of opium [3]

This makes Nixon's war on drugs look like a frolic. Is a happy country the one whose personal freedoms line the path to the gallows?

I have been solemnly warned to document this discourse with fastidious foot notes. Along with this advice is the inference that I am protecting myself and this work from litigation or cease and desist notices. So I have two choices: one, to lose my learned audience who want to trace my every quote and paraphrase to its literary source, or to lose my casual readers who have no intention of sticking with a piece of pedantry. And underneath all of this is the specter of self censorship where "one false move" – omit some attribution- and your whole work is nullified! So, I accede to scholarly formality yet want to live up to my own battle cry: occupy the language!

Freedom of speech in this alleged land of the free does not hinge on the verbalization of free thought. Precisely what happens to that speech once it is thought or once it is uttered as it works its way from the lips or printed word of the speaker may indeed embargo it from the society it was intended to address. The torrent of talking points aimed at drowning out our voices, the preponderance of tabloid news and analysis from major media, the lies and snake oil oaths taken by political candidates has left democratic discourse in shambles. No wonder I think of it as a hostile takeover of our language itself.

Next time you hear one media pundit interviewing another instead of calling upon an independent scholar, prominent author or even man on the street who is not pre-packaged into a brief sound bite, just consider public discourse to now be living in exile.

PUNCTUATION

In the old west we punctuated our sentences with bullets
leaving a brief pause for desperate pleading.

Wars grew out of well-crafted rhetoric
the generals punctuating their orders
with bombs and invasions.

The President stood before us with a worried expression
promising not to punctuate history
with mass murder and occupations.

Our children paraded to school in rank and file
prepared to learn proper punctuation
spelling
syntax
the manipulation of verbs and nouns
debate in preparation for condemnation
ending at times in massacre

We taught them the history of slavery
with the lives of runaways sometimes
punctuated by lynching

Gentlemen, I give you the semi-colon,
do what you will with it
I don't want a history of bullet points
not for me, my family
unknown mothers,
children with their run-on sentences

Period.

13

OBSTRUCT INJUSTICE

"... Disobedience is the true foundation of liberty.."
– Thoreau

"**G**entlemen start your computers." When the vast prison system in the U.S. was increasingly privatized and expanded under President Clinton, to be stoked by the Omnibus Crime Bill as if Ronald Reagan had never left office, the incentive of prisons–for–profits became all about filling up all those beds in all those state of the art prisons around the country. And to accomplish that we needed to penetrate new criminal markets like marijuana smokers, traffic ticket shirkers and "three strikes you're out" losers whose third strike might be lifting a roll of duct tape from True Value. This is the height of institutional tyranny: when society no longer needs the steel-jawed image of a dictator staring back at you as you bow to the power of a corrupt authoritarian state.

Technofascism consolidates its power in part through the authority of the job description; the one that codifies the "stress positions" you place your prisoner in regardless of what the Universal Declaration of Human Rights and Geneva Conventions have to say about it; the one that keeps you fabricating that tar sands pipeline to hell; the one that has you foreclosing on an old woman's house three payments to mortgage pay-off. You bet you have lost your humanity the paradox being: the system has been made rather perfect through minimizing human interaction, as you gradually become an anonymous mild mannered institutional tyrant. Expressions like "malignant normality" come to mind.

The twisted architecture of modern American prisons emerged in part from the essays and diagrams of British philosopher, Jeremy Bentham (1748-1832).[1]

A prison nation presents the forced stasis that kills democratic life and warns all of those who have eluded its gaping jowls that punishment is ever closing in behind us. In a prison state, the word security is code for "order at gun point." That is why the NRA under Trump danced in the streets.

Unjust laws are not only there to ensnare the innocent but to be nullified and corrected by an activist population that is willing to stand with those most affected, in the streets, the courthouse steps, the social media, schools, family dinner tables and so on.

It is no coincidence that Gandhi, Martin Luther King, Medgar Evers, JFK and RFK, all of whom were assassinated, were standing in the way of a fully corrupt and unscrupulous establishment, vestiges of which remain with us today, whether manifested as assassination or election theft or concoctions of wars domestic and foreign.

By following the major media today, one would have little awareness of the underlying anti-war fiber of American society. Vietnam in its early stages was somewhat credible to an unsuspecting public but once worn off, American gullibility morphed into a full voiced protest movement, which by 1969 was raising the high decibel anti-war demonstrations to the level of political mandate, even in Washington.

It could be argued that justice in America died on day one of Columbus' incursion into the New World; that injustice was the very corner stone of policies that lead to the systematic genocide of indigenous peoples; that injustice was the bed rock of the slave economy; that injustice was the engine of post Civil War life in America with its continued racist culture; that the shaming and demoralization of the southern states only served to perpetuate all of the hatreds and bigotries associated with social injustice. It was as if all descendants of slaveholders were swept up in the sins of their great grandfathers. Justice can never be established through war or any form of aggression for that matter.

Returning to the eighteenth century philosopher Jeremy Bentham, he had applied principles of technology wedded to architecture to inform his architecture of the ideal prison. In a macabre institution he dubbed "panopticon," a central observation tower looks out at a multi-story structure built in a circular shape so that guards could see into all of the prisoner's cells simultaneously at all times of day or night.[2]

Although his ideologically depraved idea never was fully realized it shows how prepared the authoritarians of the time were to depriving people of their fundamental right to privacy. How ecstatic Bentham and his contemporaries might have been to have lived to see the age of mass surveillance as it now exists in activities like project Prism in which communications from all over the world are intercepted through the primary transmission devices with absolutely no FISA protections.

We need to keep in mind that Nazism represents the apotheosis of order, not the kind of order that presides over living organisms, but the kind that is at war with natural diversity and the infinite continuum of relationship, human to human, life to earth and the inter-animation of elements themselves.

DAPL, the Dakota Access Pipeline appropriately dubbed the "black snake" continues to bring out the best and worst in human interaction with the planetary paradise on which we reside. Climate justice has never been better represented than by the intertribal and interracial actions around DAPL which serve as an example of the blessings of much needed social activism and visionary zeal for all people.

INNOCENCE

We now learn
that matter in the universe
is aligned in a grid,
that each molecule knows its mark
as if order came first,
that the stars know the moment of our birth
as if knowledge came first,
that each canvas knows what it wants to become
as if image came first,
that the tiger knows when to strike
as if power came first,
that prayer is answered
as if God came first.
And as all systems fail
all gods flee,
all stars fall
and as knowledge is overrun by innocence,

something else comes into being...prepare.

14

THE CONVENIENCE OF RUSSIA

"Putin on the Ritz"

–JK

The first lesson of "empire building 101" in a post-colonial world, for a country that studies history through a pin hole aperture, is that when you cannot legitimately colonize, you invent a pretext to invade for varied other reasons. The renowned "forty five minutes to attack" –Tony Blair- accompanied by a deadly phial of anthrax echoes over the land like the sound check at a punk rock concert. So goes Iraq. Oil and gas are never mentioned. Moreover, in Afghanistan lie unquestionably, a trillion dollars worth of rare earth metals that the technology industry lusts after.[1] What better excuse for neo-colonization and occupation qua so-called humanitarian intervention?

The mad geniuses who invented the cold war came up with the perfect morphology from classic colonialism to neocon invasion-ism. Call it what you like. Big profits are to be made in aerospace and munitions with the occasional nuclear aircraft carrier darkening a harbor near you.

For now the race is on to expand our imperialistic reach if merely to beat our worthy competitors to the punch. Seven hundred billion for defense and competition from both Russia and China conspire to escalate aggression in the worldwide markets we serve and claim to protect. Game on; this all transpiring under the evil eye of global elites, ever the war profiteers, the depression makers, predatory bankers, you name it. Ultimately the role of America globally is also placed in a much larger context of a New World Order as first articulated by Bush senior.

It's one thing to cast a wide net in congressional hearings, investigations, grand juries, blue ribbon committees, prompted reportage and so called opposition research, but come on guys, after two years this "The Russians Did It" tabloid reality show is getting a bit stale. There is plenty of collusion to go around from both major political parties including the Dems if you bring in the Clintons…plural. And there are many extra-governmental actors in Russo-American business relationships that avoid state channels entirely in their business dealings. Any major crimes here?

And as for the much vaunted Russian election meddling: if we put together a play list of home-grown election manipulations and out-and-out thefts of our democratic process it would include Gore Vs Bush 2000 in Florida, the history of district gerrymandering, "black box" voting in un-auditable proprietary machines, unlimited dark money and PAC money in elections, voter stripping and caging by private contractors, abuse of voter I.D. requirements, derailing the Bernie movement from inside the party, to list just a few. So with "friends like these" who needs foreign enemies? I for one find it difficult to rationalize the benefit of a Trump bump by the Russians based on the aggressive ferocity and cold war brinkmanship of his administration alone. What we now have on the world stage are two nations held in the grip of their respective oligarchies- yes the U.S.A. too- that have every incentive to hack each other as their respective populations shrivel in power.

Admittedly, Vladimir Putin's countenance is a central casting director's dream. For Putin to not have been written into the next James Bond movie as the arch nemesis is a huge mistake. But to attribute evil motives to the real Putin is the height of cold war opportunism. The messaging from the American side is clear with every word a sucker punch aimed at provoking what should be a peaceful competitor into knee-jerk militancy.

Concurrently, Ukraine's right wing Risorgimento has coaxed all of the neo Nazis out of their caves into the light; a consequence no doubt overlooked by Mr. Obama and his advisor Victoria Nuland who were mingling with the merry villagers of Kiev handing out orange scarves on street corners.[2]

In the modern history of military contest and conflict, regional wars simply seem to suffer from unreliable shelf lives. Even Afghanistan became more and more untenable as an existential threat to our hallowed shores. The super powers, on the other hand, have a global influence and competitive reach that can easily be spun as aggression. China in Africa, the BRICS economic alliance which evades the U.S. dollar as the center of the economic universe, Sino Russian military might and nuclear overkill: all these are poised to bring on brinkmanship and pump up the military industrial complex. Et voila!

Meanwhile, Americans would never have set foot on the moon without some Soviet collaboration. Today, we essentially have no space station and rely on Soyuz for NASA programs. We also owe much of the research and development in space medicine to Russia's program.

It was interesting for me to personally meet First Lady Nancy Reagan in the mid-eighties as a teacher-mentor of music prodigies whose young performers received invitations to White House and U.N. events. The great effort she personally put into orchestrating the series of Reykjavik meetings between Presidents Reagan and Gorbachev marks a moment in history in which the two super powers most closely joined together in envisioning a world without nuclear weapons- a welcome anomaly in the Reagan years.[4]

In Iceland, the Soviets agreed to the double zero plan for eliminating Intermediate range nuclear weapons in Europe, as originally proposed, with Nancy's influence, by President Reagan in 1981. The Soviets also proposed to mutually build down half of the inventory of all strategic arms, including ICBMs, and agreed not to include British or French weapons in the inventory. All this was offered on the condition that the Americans put a pause on implementing strategic defenses for a ten years period in concert with SALT I. [6]

How ironic that the United States subsequently took credit for the Soviet break up as a step toward world peace when in fact it was used as the perfect pretext for returning to business as usual in the nuclear arms build up which continues today throughout the developed world. So damned if you do and damned if you don't: the cold war gets people to the disarmament table and détente sees them running full speed out the back door. This is one area where a hairline crack hardly exists between the dedicated position of Democrats and Republicans. They all want a big fuzzy enemy for Northrup Grumman to materialize every time billions are requested through their megaphones in congress.

Well, a couple of generations ago the Russians fought the last decisive battles of World War II thereby assuring a future for their allied partners for the foreseeable future. This neglected achievement highlights the complete loss of soul as well as loss of senses the American people and their ill-elected representatives have brought upon themselves and the rest of the world in the ensuing decades. At the same time, the Americans were throwing nuclear bombs out of airplanes knowing full well that documents had been prepared behind the scenes for the Japanese to agree, not to a full surrender, but a cessation of hostilities.[7] The magnitude of Harry Truman's unprecedented use of weapons of mass destruction to incinerate hundreds of thousands of innocent people is beyond measurement. How incredible is it that the time interval between Guernica and Hiroshima is a brief eight years?

And now technofascists move in where humane thinkers fear to tread. They reach out all right, with bullets and bombs and prepare for cyber warfare, intel warfare, and all the paraphernalia of faux techno-security that coalesce into the madness of empire.

What sways the results of American elections arises more from how elections are managed, candidates recruited, voters discouraged or pre-empted and how ballots mal-tabulated than how opinions are formed by the people who vote. The advanced accusation factory targeting the Russians in advance of the 2018 midterms is an orchestrated effort to distract from the work that has to be done to overhaul the corrupt duopoly running politics in this country.

On the other hand … a great nation like the United States needs and deserves a great enemy/adversary in military terms or great competitor in economic parlance. That sick state of mind finds it appealing to reach a bit into the past to cold war times in reinstating the foreign policy tried and true that enjoyed success for a couple of generations. In that devil's bargain one puts a fresh skin on a nationalism that sells much better to the American people than Trump's or even Obama's slice and dice militarism. At the same time we create the perfect distraction from our own political-social malignancy which no dark corner of government can successfully hide or obfuscate any longer.

Not since the good old days of "godless communism" have we seen a whipping up of anti Russian fervor as lead by the English speaking world and their lackey-state supporting cast. Innocent until proven guilty has been a principle tenet of Common Law since the Magna Carta. Only Orwell and the present U.S. administration has managed to fit that old dead horse with a new bridle.

15

We The People Are Not an Audience

Imagine the feeling of power an actor achieves as he plays to an audience, all facing him with rapt attention; suspending disbelief, held hostage, mute, all captives; the actor now morphing into an anchor of a TV news hour… his script: the narrative of reality that the state, the corporate sponsors, the ratings bean counters and the security spooks need delivered. The "need to know" principle, the last line of defense against whistle blowers, has now been escalated to all corporate-agenda media. And woe betides the outlier investigative reporters and ethical intellectuals who valiantly pursue the truth, at the same time, wading through mountains of disinformation that has our alleged democracy in an informational choke hold. We thought that reporters and truth seekers were oppressed in dictatorships. Well they certainly are, but in the case of the USA, we are now witnessing dictatorial control on many levels; a kind of twisted freedom to choose one's words no matter how original, while editorially controlled.

For the CIA as a powerful covert organ of the state to lose its commanding sway over the great American audience- as it were- by not being able to own the message being framed and transmitted over the major media is deemed unacceptable. Punks –as the media cast them- like Snowden, Manning, Assange and Drake loom as they grow in popularity to a near heroic degree, and simply must be reined in, if not figuratively lynched, as so many escaped slaves from the information plantation.

The courage and success of alternative media can be measured by the magnitude of the campaign against it. A truly robust democracy can certainly withstand foreign and relatively independent organizations like Al Jazeera, RT (Russian Television) and Wikileaks.org. While a growing list of reality based investigative information desks largely survive, we need to remain vigilant in opposing efforts to attack them, indeed, censor them in the corporate, government sponsored media as well as the halls of congress. Accusations by the establishment that propaganda emanates from alternative media are inverted to say the least.

So too, our population has been saturated by salvo after salvo of opinion polls. What appears as a perfectly innocent polling question on politics for example, is actually a meticulously crafted leading question that "pushes" a certain response such as "if North Korea refuses to cease development of nuclear weapons does the U.S. have the obligation to intervene with military force?" What is not provided is the prefatory remark that around a dozen nations have developed weapons of just that description and that a couple of the above refuse to sign any non-proliferation treaty, and as if that weren't enough, North Korea has shown willingness to discuss a "freeze for a freeze" where sanctions would be lifted in exchange for placing their nuclear program on hold.[1]

Hence, what is omitted from the question completely controls the outcome of the poll and creates a false impression that the people are in lock step agreement with the generals.

The corporate news media, print and pixel, are under the impression that what does not survive the twenty-four hour news cycle ceases to exist. What is more, those whose misdeeds are swept up in the media are guaranteed to wane with the new dawn like a kind of induced amnesia. This is what a Donald Trump relies on in making some of his wilder and preposterous claims and insults. Launch a war on Monday and it sinks below the awareness horizon by Friday.

Proof that the American people are treated by the power elites as nothing more than a gullible audience is present in the endless script driven nature of every media and public event taken up by our government. Even the White House press corps is carefully controlled in advance through unopposed obfuscation on the part of any federal official who faces them.

When you have a democratic constitution that clearly impedes a variety of autocratic and dictatorial tendencies of the ruling elites, all of the "exceptions to the rule" gradually take over policy making in the country. The Defense Authorization Act does an end run around congress' war making powers; presidential pardons forgive the guilty, further punishing their victims; executive orders role back environmental protections left and right; federal prohibitions like cannabis as a schedule one controlled substance, subvert states' rights; the Supreme Court nullifies the results of a state electoral process e.g. Al Gore in 2000.

In the movie "Blade Runner," and now in its sequel, the incredible realm where human and "replicant" lose the sense of differentiation between man and machine; where a sub-set of replicants develop the ability for their bodies to achieve human reproduction, we find ourselves projected into that dystopian future place where our species have surrendered to technologies that are delusionally positioned as surpassing human frailty and emotionality et al.

Ronald Reagan and Donald Trump are both American entertainment products representing the best we have in visual mediocrity. The very fact of their success in politics speaks to the entertainment monstrosity we might call the big electoral TV show. The Clinton's, in their own way, continue to work the pixel palace to the hilt as well. One might cite the mammoth corporate backed bankrolls that drive their campaigns. Meanwhile, Hollywood is kept happy knowing that the great politicians continue to pass through their portals. It would be remiss not to mention the fakery that goes into our well-televised political debates and party conventions. Just reflect on the immense post election issue of war and peace brought to us by the Trump administration- an issue that was nowhere to be found in the debates.

The underestimating of the American electorate is part and parcel of the corporate media agenda for the people. There is every reason to remain extremely cynical about our dominant political duopoly. Our reality, our history, our morality, our humanism have all been assaulted. The mainstream media remain their accomplices. One way for people of integrity to seek revenge from the MSM would be to invent a new hall of fame and awards event that calls out the worst among us be they high elected officials or commoners. The Annual Hand Basket Awards would essentially be a people's choice event, perhaps on a dedicated website. AHBA, as an annual event could eventually get around to most of the hideous among us who are taking us straight to "hell in a hand basket." My own nominees would be just that, my own personal list, of no particular influence in this intended popular poll. But here we go with a few: Donald J Trump, Debbie Wasserman Schultz, Joe Arpaio , Lloyd Blankfein.

Perfect crimes and ethical derelictions are likely the ones we have never heard of. Once an individual disappears into the labyrinth of technology there is likelihood that they will lose their identity, their personality, their face, their name, to say nothing of losing their soul. Moreover, the opportunity to disassociate from their chosen mode of evil doing is accommodated brilliantly in cyberspace. A bank of transfixed faces highlighted in the bluish glow of computer screens, each looking out at images transmitted by video gimbals bristling from predator drones is not a very charismatic setting for the deadly drama of a bloody battlefield. And yet, the drone body count mounts on a daily basis along with the gruesomely high proportion of deaths of bystanders. In a sense this scenario is perfect in its insanity in that it perfects the removal of direct human interaction with the enemy. A twisted notion of professionalism in which an individual is scripted by their superiors to commit acts and speak words that bare no relationship with the true identity of the actor is the perfect tool of technofascism. Legions of self-respecting scientists should be sitting in on the Pentagon steps in round the clock vigil to demand the word science be taken out of military science. This just in: Psychologists will be collaborating with torturers in Guantanamo. Stay tuned.

This brutal yet pathologically emotionless state of modern military combat in the name of the war on terror did not emerge out of a vacuum. Nearly all armies are locked into behavioral grids wherein personal volition is eviscerated in favor of the "well oiled machine." This generates a mantel of "higher purpose" and individual deniability over acts which in any other context look like murder. But what did it mean to carpet bomb innocent populations in Viet Nam? How did it feel to torture prisoners in Abu Ghraib? At least in the last century, fascism sported brown shirts and grimacing faces. Now it thrives in an environment of amorality and alienation.

One need not make a case for the many modes of social control required to run a technofascist state. Is that Facebook comment really your unique view of something or is it an expression of a deeply seeded groupthink that is being shaped by the chosen medium of communication? Twitter does it, Snap Chat, Linked In; they all manipulate the public into a state of self-censoring conformity.

In order for some marvelous software to construct its beautifully colored pie charts of you, me and everyone else, humans simply need to feed the beast data like so many zookeepers. And the chart interacting with an AI program fed by humans, will start calling the shots in the private and public sectors: profiling customers, informing customized advertising chains and pop ups, the operations that humans used to do in marketing and business sales. Artificial intelligence is the terminal blow to the primacy of the human mind and the true spirit of free enterprise.

"All media exist to invest our lives with artificial perceptions and arbitrary values," saith Marshall Mcluhan.

There is a difference between opening up a newspaper to a particular article and listening/watching broadcast media. The print article is only a narrative, read at the reader's pace and comprehension. Broadcast media captivate the senses, determine the tempo, the emotional curve, the emphasis and sequence of everything being delivered with no opening for reflection or selection or an alternate stream of consciousness. The media tend to overly spin and "package summarize" their content leaving no breathing space for personal opinion.

Mr. McLuhan is the one person who is capable of introducing self-doubt in my own polemic against technology and politics. That is why my interviews with media spin-doctors may be somewhat sparse. I trust that books were not particularly in his crosshairs in his attacks on the media.

I Bend My Ink

I bend my ink toward perfect worlds
scripture appears on stone
where faces have never shone

I gather verse in nets of light
liberating song
to rescue ruined dreams
of a drowning night

Since our histories have twisted
all that is to be,
I pause before opening books

Pause to read the epic twists
that flow along the branches of a tree
the winged throb of honey bee

If you see me stand alone
empty handed
silent

Know that constellations
crowd my thoughts

and sense my blood

16

TWISTED

If only those smart people who decided it was a neat idea to split the atom in order to boil water, incinerate great swathes of humanity, seek out lesions in pipelines and flaws in intestines, had thought intently about the consequences of their actions, the doomsday clock might be paused a bit more than two minutes 'til midnight.

So there is technology and there is technology: one malignant the other beneficial. And once you add the ingredient of long-time vested economic interest into these technologies, you have a recipe for distortion of most of what goes into making constructive progress. The energy industry has known for generations that it was hitching its wagon to the cliff racing scene in Rebel Without a Cause: all the machismo of a race to the precipice, but this time with us all going over the edge.

Virtually the day after Albert Einstein endorsed the use of nuclear fission to construct the atom bomb, he began his years of remorse – very outspoken at that – in which he wrote about a world beyond weapons of mass destruction.

"You cannot simultaneously prevent and prepare for war" is how I recall the quote.[1]

Now we pivot to the use of communications technology to invade the inner thoughts of modern humanity in an attempt to engineer our actions, our opinions and worse yet, to legally suppress free thought and free speech. The Defense Authorization Act and associated Use of Force policies, upheld by both major parties in power under their respective presidents, has been paving the way to the dark side of Alexander Graham Bells' magical invention with no end in sight. Total surveillance is here, riding on a generation of cutting-edge snoop technologies. If I may bring in merry old England as example, about half a million-security cameras are deployed around London. New software, which recognizes faces and walking gaits, has been deployed and scarcely opposed by the citizenry. It's all working like a charm.[2]

A Google server farm interrupts that same Columbia Gorge scenic view. Actually, "farm" is a good descriptor, at least in sheer floor space, acres of industrial space, erected to do nothing but produce a million pages of search results and millions of products and services to buy in a well-researched half a second for every entry in the search window. Must we now jump to that ultimate scenario of a single organization having the power to sort, rank and censor everything that pops up on a search? And what a great way it is to keep all those kooky conspiracy theorists who think that the power elite have something to hide, questioning their own sanity. The practice of exercising control over controversy itself is abundantly obvious. As stated in a Counterpunch article of August 2017:

"Under its new so-called anti-fake-news program, Google algorithms have in the past few months moved socialist, anti-war, and progressive websites from previously prominent positions in Google searches to positions up to 50 search result pages from the first page, essentially removing them from the search results any searcher will see. CounterPunch, World Socialist Website, Democracy Now, American Civil liberties Union, Wikileaks are just a few of the websites which have experienced severe reductions in their returns from Google searches. World Socialist Website, to cite just one example, has experienced a 67% drop in its returns from Google since the new policy was announced."[3]

This conversion of Google into an algorithmic censorship engine is no trivial development. Google searches are currently a primary means by which workers and other members of the public seek information about their lives and their world. Every effort must be made to combat this serious infringement of the basic rights of freedom of speech and freedom of press. But now we find that the number of Google search results that are screened out for opposing the media message machine is on the increase.

One need not make a case for the many modes of social control required in a technofascist state. Is that Facebook comment really your unique view of something or is it an expression of a deeply seeded group think that is being shaped by the chosen medium of communication? Twitter does it, Snap chat, Linked In; they all finesse the public into a state of self censorship and conformity.

And Net neutrality is now threatened by the FCC promoting what might be called "net centrality" where the control of the media by and for the few is being reenacted on the information highway.

Getting back to the opening scenario of this chapter extolling the geological and riparian wonders in which I live. Fracking anyone? If you are one so fortunate to live in Oklahoma, you now must be getting the feeling that terra firma has become terra tremora: earthquakes delivered fresh to your door every day. Fracking destabilizes the great cavities in the geological strata as it mines for natural gas. The technology of fracking has been promoted around the world by North Americans. The only silver lining to fracking is the launching of Josh Fox's film making career. And do place your bets on the fact that fracking has erased the fantasized political aisle across which our alleged representatives reach. Now go and make your own sentence without ending in a preposition.

17

DEMOCRACY NOW AND THEN

Conspiracy Theory or historical correction

Well, may I say that yet another American stentorian icon gets no apology from me in authoring this diatribe on the criminal negligence involved in unbridled technofascism. It's one thing to parrot the hackneyed meme, "conspiracy theorists," but for progressive investigative journalists to avoid any discussion of potential major conspiracies themselves in the face of the irrefutability of evidence plays into the real conspiracy itself. Face it, "controlled demolition" has a certain ring of appropriateness vis a vis the World Trade Center collapses- especially building seven. Now go look for that topic in all but the remote fringes of the media.

Or when a major mass murder such as the Las Vegas Mandalay Bay massacre is followed by a complete filtering of public access to evidence, third party archiving, in-depth investigative interviewing. It's as if a huge red –or false- flag is being waved in our faces. Pay heed ye alternative information dispensers. Ye too may be manipulated. I don't want to single out a particular alternative news and discussion organization in the media although there is an obvious pun in the above chapter title!

We now know that the military demons assembled around JFK had hatched a plan to carry out a false flag attack on Miami and blame Castro. And of course the plan for full invasion of Cuba to follow by our own version of "Condor Legion" was advanced to JFK by the generals, only to be thwarted by the Commander in Chief. [1]

This is an object lesson in what treachery our country is capable of. And what's this I see in a tabloid, of all things, while standing in the check out line at the super market this morning?:

"OSWALD WAS CIA." Easy to dismiss from a tabloid, but... ...

Gulf of Tonkin: done! Iran Contra: done! The October Surprise: Done! Florida presidential vote in 2000: done! And when we add up the proven examples of in house conspiracies (with or without JFK, RFK and MLK), our alternative news organizations had better get crackin'. With all due respect to issues of the environment, police brutality, gender and economic injustice, we have yet to crack open our deep state – with the help of a free media- and the real power elite who occupy the penthouses of the New World Disorder. So with a jump starter named Assange under de facto arrest in a London low rise, how can we miss?

I often wonder why Noam Chomsky admittedly has no interest in finding out who planned and executed 9/11. Strange indeed… given that he is distinguished in his area of science. Yet to not challenge the canard that jet fuel collapsed the buildings in a matter of seconds essentially throws the Architects and Engineers for 9/11 Truth, some of whom have been his MIT colleagues, under the trolley. And yes, does a leading American leftist intellectual need to hit every perfect sphere over the fence? Maybe… maybe not.

I worry that this diatribe leads to nothing constructive from the author as a remedy aside for exclamations like "oh well" and "it is what it is." But that's where you get the author wrong. Here I sit proclaiming for starters that we go beyond getting money out of politics, meaning that we get the parties themselves out of politics!

It has been proven again and again from time immemorial that science thrives best in a democratic setting. Just ask Copernicus and Galileo what the nullifying effect was of the prelates in collusion with the state on their very great scientific work. In the present day, the finest minds in fields like climate science, sustainable energy, even evolution are summarily lined up by political firing squads who unleash a barrage of invective, barbarous legislation and underhanded deregulation. The valiant work of data collection which tells the truth about how successful our nation is at health, education, welfare, peace making and dealing with disasters is kept in a dark closet. Distribution of wealth, access to good health care and affordable housing are all left to the "free market" which inevitably benefit the upper classes of our society. Here is where the Europeans are leaving us far behind in a fool's paradise.

We are in an historic period in which a hostile takeover of the truth itself has been advanced to a place of primacy in the daily existence of our country. National Public Radio and PBS in the way they conduct business, are antithetical to public interest in both vision and present structure. The Kochs, McDonalds and big pharma are frequent sponsors of public broadcasting and certainly cast a broad shadow over the parameters of content and political influence therein.[2]

The Democratic party have counted on NPR to keep the business model of American politics in status quo and are adept at using public broadcasting to avoid certain topics from being brought up such as their own corrupt DNC. No, Donald Trump by example is not lifting all of the opposition boats. On the contrary, he is taking the whole flotilla down with him. Independent voters are the only constituency in our society who are capable of evaluating and supporting individual candidates for office who may not be tainted by monetized politics.

We are at a juncture in which any given politician could trade in his/her shirt for a team jersey advertising the corporation or billionaire donor who put them in office. And the politically comatose population that go along with all of this have been so underinformed and so lied to that we might be looking at a veritable, irremediable decline and fall of our failed experiment in democracy.

Technofascism will take science and technology -as mankind has known it- down with it into the black hole of its own making. One step along the way, the role that politics will play, is best described in this pithy epigram of Marshal Mcluhan:

"Politics will eventually be replaced by imagery. The politician will... abdicate in favor of his image, because the image will be much more powerful than he could ever be."[4]

And don't you worry one bit, once the politician is fully pixelated, there are plenty of staff advisors and manager types around to run the government while an entrenched minority of TV bots gather around their silicon sensoria to lend it credibility.

Among our greatest displays of participatory democracy are the spontaneous popular actions across the country against war, corruption, racism and gun violence. With the leadership of high schoolers, the marches and walkouts against our derelict congress and its NRA overlords present a drastic dose of reality that is there for objective reporting by the mainstream media- or not... Our hallowed second amendment remains one of the most cognitively twisted documents imaginable. When the document was written, the definition of arms referred to single shot rifles, manually cocked pistols, powder horns and the like; what is not contemplated are spray action assault rifles, fragmentation weapons, ballistic missiles nor space based laser weapons for that matter. The diabolical multiplier affect of weapons of mass murder must be factored into the interpretation of our constitution along with the term "well regulated militia." This all lurks at ground zero of the technofascist killing field.

Success

We failed and everyone who searched with us failed.
who tired of the trade
who threw up walls
centered and stooled themselves
shut their eyes to open up their souls
and learned the tying of shoes by Braille

who set out in a shell upon the wave
to catch a swell
but slopped to shore
and ended groping for another grape

who taught stuttering mouths to issue reverences
to minked popes
and popped their ears riding home in the plane,
failed with licked thumb raised finger and seminary tea

and we were all there
whole legions of laureate geniuses
dazzlingly blind
practicing the walk
learning the language
trying to save the world.

18

REGIME CHANGE BEGINS AT HOME

"Every country must be absolutely free to adopt the type of economic,
political and social system that it considers convenient"
                                                    – Fidel Castro

I have gotten to the point of narcissistically quoting myself while Bartlett and Shakespeare and other manuals of purloined literacy lie strewn across my office floor. A couple of quips that have reached bumper sticker status are "obstruct injustice" and "let's make war a controlled substance."

I still await the impending rear end collision as some hapless motorist loses himself in the new mystical land I advocate for; a land beyond imperialist wars, lopsided looted wealth, beyond contempt for ethnicity, poverty, intellect, earthiness, the gender continuum, climate justice and all the rest of it. Are we on board for no parties at all? No Dems- sorry you succumbed to super pacs, and the permanent war economy as you eviscerated Bernie, no Reps- sorry... so many ways to fill in the details.

So much of our lives is dictated from above by forces unseen that will never relinquish their power unless it is torn from their grasp -non-violently of course-. Given my own and many people's commitment to non-violence, one might vote for the best candidates many of whom run outnumber Republicans and Democrats. The slogan "money out of politics" misses the point. The sin lies with the permissible scale of the donation. Long before the Bernie Sanders run it was Howard Dean mounting an online fifty state campaign of small contributions: the same man who was dumped for not cozying up to big corporate sponsors then paradoxically condescended to become a major lobbyist for big pharma via chairmanship of the Democratic party. So no free passes for either party as they cave to new lows in corruption and chicanery in the last couple of decades.

A trend in American society that has set in so gradually and subtly as to be unnoticed even by political scientists is the replacement of patriotism by nationalism. To accept patriotism in its wider definition which includes not just what Marines do on the shores of Tripoli –irony intended – but what a William Binney, former NSA intel officer does when he blows the whistle on the NSA for constitutional crimes or when a million people hit the streets against the invasion of Iraq or the Vietnam war or a whole activist society pops up in the wilderness of North Dakota to save our environment or when Colin Kaepernick drops to a knee while everyone else in the football stadium is practicing, yes, you guessed it, nationalism; indeed to accept patriotism in whole cloth is a problem for the state ergo the pivot toward nationalism wherein the role of patriotic opposition, whistle blowing, occupy movements, peaceful resistance and all the rest is crushed by that same state.

You know we have a regime in the White House when flotillas of war ships are sent half way round the world to keep the peace. You know you live under a regime when all of the best efforts of popular humanitarian organizations are systematically dismantled before our eyes. You know you live in a regime when the President is given a free pass on violating the Geneva Conventions, the Nuremberg Principles and the dicta of the International Criminal Court on a daily basis. You know you live under a regime when the society around you seems frozen in a negative panic –as happens to passengers in a plane going down. We surely have a regime when there are enough redacted lines in state documents to populate a library of blackened books the size of the National Archives.

The current data on positions held by Republicans over Democrats, Independents, Greens and Libertarians in every level of government don't tell the whole story of the political will of the people in this country. The expression "left coast" is well taken since with virtually all higher political positions held by other than Republicans in California, Oregon and Washington, figures like Jeff Merkley, Jay Inslee and Jerry Brown make it seem as if the Republicans "have no power here" as stated in the Wizard of Oz. At the same time, former "Berners," some inside or outside the Democratic party are poised to run for down ballot positions from PTAs to city councils to state houses and everything in between in up coming elections. As for Sanders himself, the follies of his party have certainly taken a toll on him, but I swear, the man still looks as fit as a retired track star, which he is.

For about a year now in the town that I live in the Columbia Gorge I had been rallying with a group of committed involved citizens in opposition to the crack down on immigrants, mostly Latino, who are part of the cultural and economic back bone of our community. I personally stood in front of the detention center –also functioning as the four county jail in the region - several days each week holding big signs with messages like: ICE OUT, DE-ICE and ICE FREE ZONE. This refers to federal Immigration and

Customs Enforcement which is conducting sweeps of immigrant workers throughout the northwest. From our point of view, immigrants whose only infraction is incomplete or wholly undocumented status should not be held in the general population of a high security institution at all. This crack down smacks of racist tyranny or proto-fascism.

So here we are, reminiscing about democracy and liberty, one man one vote, innocent until proven guilty, the Magna Carta and so on. Yet perhaps, in truth, we have never attained the level of democracy that was promised by our forbears. We had a Civil War, but slavery quickly morphed into forms of servitude that remain in place until today.

And so humiliated was the losing side of the war that it should surprise no one that so much super patriotic racial hate is emanating from the south; this in combination with pockets of bigotry in the north brought a slice of hell to our nation's first racially diverse presidency.

My somewhat radical friends have never been more energized to get out and be active; to go door to door, demonstrate in the streets, write a letter to the editor. Political parties be damned; the architects and captains of technofascism are going down!

Powerful political leaders in our country, having failed completely in prosecuting war crimes for the invasions of Iraq and Afghanistan now must earn a spot on the exclusive "guest list " of the proceedings of the International Criminal Court in The Hague.

We now know, how hack-able electronic voting machines hold sway out there in precincts all over the country. There is no telling the number of elections that are being stolen anywhere, anytime through digital intervention. Paper ballots a pre-technological approach is one cure. We also know that the FCC is gravitating toward making media monopolies even easier to grow and maintain as well as creating two tiers of the internet with unregulated control being given to the big players.[1] So many of the current regulatory agencies are regimes within regimes with corruption and collusion operating up and down the line.

This may be the life we are used to; the life we have come to know. But we don't need to accept regime rule until the day it appears in the constitution. And we need never acquiesce to technofascism, but rather, oppose it with every fiber of our being.

"If you want to change your nation, change your village. "If you want to change the world, first change your heart."[2]

– Confucius.

Aggression

Uphill we walk
Watched by the birds
Who don't name us
Lumbering through mud
Snapping twigs
An awkward species

We're watched by time that doesn't tell us
Doesn't change
We are the hands on the dial
We are escaping sand
And alarms at dawn

We're watched by the murdered eyes of innocents
Who don't know us
Don't know their slayers
Slaughtered but not conquered
Subdued but not controlled

We walk as the skies open to a storm
Rivulets
Then streams
Weeping down the mountain
Like backward time

19

SOCIAL MEDIA AS WHITE NOISE

"This is the way world ends, not with a bang, ... but a twitter"
— T.S. Eliot/J.K.

Now that earthling eyeballs have all been taken over by little off-shore manufactured screens; now that cars have been transformed into lethal weapons by craven texters; now that the former President has a Twitter implant in the only remaining lobe of his brain, it is time to declare the social media, the Internet and related technologies to be instruments of narcissism. While some of our favorite truth warriors reside on the web, their share of bandwidth is infinitesimal compared with the relentless dross to which we addict ourselves. The inventors of the information highway never intended a thousand lanes in both directions with no off ramps.

The main saving grace to everyone walking around with cell phones is the ability to witness and record the brutal treatment of our fellow citizens in real time. So if Eric Garner ends up not receiving adequate justice, the pictures deliver a different and lasting message to history. Another silver lining to the use of devices is coming with the increased use of body cams in police departments. This will make it increasingly difficult for so called police internal investigations to keep all of the evidence in a black box away from public view. One hopes that the revelations of general communications interception by the NSA and their private contractors –via Ed Snowden- will goad our congress into doing more than standing at attention, saluting all things constitutionally dodgy.

One of the best prospects of all for social media lies in the future of free and fair elections –as Sanders writ large- where super PACs are outlawed and all sorts of candidates emerge from the redwood forests to the gulf stream waters. Without that kind of sea change in our political system, we'll have to revert to pitch forks and flaming torches.

We are all aware that the Arab Spring began in an open market in Tunis with a self-immolating activist, an angry crowd and a cell phone. Well, short of using a fossil fuel for a suicide, I would not rule out such a promise for the virtual witnessing round the world of extraordinary events in society as they happen. I was particularly struck by the use of a video drone at Standing Rock in North Dakota during the DAPL ongoing uprising.

The fact that the tar sands pipeline issue survives in court is thanks in part to the brilliant videography and reportage at ground zero from the likes of Josh Fox of "Gasland" fame.[1]

Donald Trump's use of Twitter to manipulate the masses pursuant to and after the election of '16 is a pre-emptive strike against what is left of the White House reporter's scrum, reporters in print, network TV, on-line and worldwide cable. It is the perfect tool of a dictatorial personality-something Mussolini would have relished.

The loss of privacy goes with the territory when it comes to human cyber-activity. Did it have to be this way? Is this all about the profit motive behind deep marketing, coupled with the stampeding profits in the area of surveillance? Or are we seeing the advent of a full scale social engineering campaign wherein the state will impose a low intensity conformity on us all setting us up for a truly Orwellian future?

Justin Rosenstein , the Silicon Valley scion who created the "like" button on Facebook has now come out in complete opposition to the mass captivity our little screens have created around us. The funneling of that very addictive behavior into a big marketing and financial internment complex with invisible walls and watch towers. …makes you want to tunnel out.[2]

20

TECHNOLOGIES OF EXTINCTION

"Data compression becomes idea compression, becomes experience compression, becomes a pixelated life"

– JK

Yes, there are those who would blame the sun for Icarus' death; those that blame the "too many trees" for climate fires, not to mention all those teeming mouths to feed to be blamed for famine. And now, at the threshold of the looming extinction of our species, all of the perennial rationalizations for it not being caused by human fallibility are being rolled out like Model Ts off the assembly line.; not by everyone of course, but by the resource extractors, arms manufacturers, transportation guzzlers, evangelical "in God we trusters" and all purveyors of resentment toward authentic science and the very seat of intelligence in our society. What is equally calamitous is the growing belief in the hand basket of ideas for saving our species through technology itself. Be not shocked when some PhD entrepreneur figures out a way to cool down the sun! But we must ask the question first, what role has technology played historically in the planetary crisis in which we find ourselves today? We need to enquire as well, how we failed to make changes, corrections and improve practices long known to reek havoc on the environment and human health. Is corrupt capitalism and rampant industrialization explanation enough?

Particularly in western societies, innovation, "neat ideas," patents, are the pre-eminent form in which we solve global problems. But just as the human immune system is strengthened somewhat through exposure to pathogens, rushing in with a fist full of syringes may likely miss that one strain of flu that takes us down.

'No time to act as if minor adjustments in things like fuel economy, smoke stack scrubbers and telecommuting are sufficient to stop our climate avalanche mid slope. There are not enough band aids laid end to end to circle the globe even if it could make a difference.

Now is the time to be most wary of opportunistic inventors and scientists baring gifts. Now is the time to get the stain of progress out of sustainability. In any geological epoch, cataclysms of nature are bound to occur. Conclusive proof of the continued viability of life forms on the planet lies in the incalculable variety of species, some terrestrial, some water born, some suspended in air for a lifetime. On the microbial level, species adapt and selectively evolve in the most stressful climatic conditions imaginable. It's the big guys that bite the dust. Anthropomorphism has had its chance. To think that supposedly sane people now look to space for deliverance of our species including some of the most successful businessmen like Bezos, Musk and Branson ... (this sentence is better left dangling so readers supply their own ending). In the meantime we can ring the whole Florida promontory with sea walls all we want as Caribbean islands one by one quietly sink beneath the waves.

So we start by joining every effort out there that may appear to be radical in nature but in fact supports nature herself. We slap on bumper stickers on our previously anonymous cars that say things like, "end fracking" and "keep fossil fuels in the ground."

We enroll in movements and social media sites that advocate completely reinventing our economies of consumption, fashion driven innovation, material excess, pervasive disposability, the mountains of waste, the oceanic islands of plastic, even the overkill of kill in our military arsenals. And the pipelines everywhere: fracked gas, tar sands oil and the mile long coal and oil trains have fomented growing populist movements each day. We get out in the streets on short notice, predominantly peacefully and non violent but in the MLK sense of not just standing down easily.

Without question good education is at the heart of every step in the path toward learning how to rescue our species and others who are caught in this vortex of our creation. For me, education has led to everything from protesting nuclear energy and weaponry, to transportation to home conservation as well as one of my favorites: recipes in the kitchen. Surprise, surprise, no one will get me to eat another smidgen of farmed meat knowing that gallons of water go into the extruding of one burger. Domestic cattle manufacture methane, supply fetid collection pools with limitless toxic sludge, inject our veins with the remains of antibiotics lavished upon the cattle who might otherwise be killed by the sheer stress of captivity and so on.

Thermonuclear weapons are surely the greatest draconian achievement of technology's dark side. Somewhat more subtle are the proliferation of technologies that diagnose cancers and other civilization caused diseases while contributing little to actual cures. Being told our DNA predisposes us to certain diseases is fine, but no resources go to getting the crap out of processed foods. There is always the profit incentive in hyper technologies as well as the raison d'etre of many research campuses which are on the take from industries that profit from their imprimatur. Real progress requires circumspection, retrospection and vision.

The poor innocent tourist who is just waking up to the realization that his round trip to Perth Australia will dump thousands of pounds of hydrocarbons into the atmosphere is unwittingly trapped in an industry, which frankly, has been told time and time again that it is a contributor of as much as much as 10% of the total man made greenhouse emissions. "Wu Weh" saith the Taoist scholars, which is like me saying "for God's sake," cancel the trip, you should know better! Externalities are killer.

A new kind of battle: the battle of the reality makers; the paid journalists who convey the message of their partners in business, has been joined. In the other corner we have the truth diggers, the interceptors, the whistle blowers and the general on line commentators; along with John Q Public and his gallant band. Both sides are fully invested in and surrounded by technology which is just as at home in virtual reality as in reality itself – what is left of it.

Aftermath

There have been un-kept promises
Through the centuries
To deliver a Messiah,

Promises of lands never never
Knights heroic
Princesses of the dance

Fields of divine bounty
Now crowded into a snapshot
That lies upon the table
Of the abandoned room

Where once we slept
Perhaps like Jesus' family
In the morning of the advent
Of a new world

Where we had come to re-write
The stories that kept us enscriptured
In silent procession through the centuries

Our own voices now unlocked
From their cruel cages
Recapturing the stars
Beauty in the heavens
Not made special for us

Here upon our wandering speck
In the galaxy of light

Oh appear, appear sweet apparitions,
Saints, angels, givers of light!
Inhabit our dreams
Animate our dance.
We are here to witness thee,
As you rise and set with the sun!

AFTERMATH II

Peace is bad for business"

– J.K.

The engine of our permanent war machine is fueled by armed conflict complete with a whole host of well crafted and communicated pretexts and messages qua propaganda as justification. And even in the most bona fide flagrant acts of aggression, in violation of Nuremberg, Geneva and the Universal Declaration of Human Rights, no state actors have gone to jail or even been tried in International Criminal Court; not Tony Blair, Colin Powell, the Bushes, Obama and on and on. So why now should a Trump and his lieutenants have any reason to take pause in acting upon thoroughly unsubstantiated, uninvestigated incidents it claims call for U.S. led armed responses and invasions?

Demonization by race, nationality, economic system, perceived menace from abroad –subliminal at times- become the go-to rationales for maintaining standing armies, weapons inventories, dedicated national defense budgets, weapons of mass destruction. There can never be enough allegedly legitimate political/military conflicts to support an institution the size and perpetuity of the Pentagon without an unspoken mandate to substantiate or fabricate the need for continuous war mongering wherever and whenever opportunities arise. This requires whole swathes of humanity to be declared evil in this expanding market place of aggression and "haters" of America and of western life. Imagine every man woman and child in a remote Afghanistan village being judged guilty in the eye of a drone high up in the air, then executed in a due-process void. Imagine every implement of defense of a sovereign state being locked on as "enemy" targets by weapons of full spectrum dominance deployed by U.S. forces and their mercenaries. Imagine the twisted Orwell-icing of the term "good guys" as we man eight hundred U.S. military installations around the world as part of a defense budget holding wealth equal or greater than the next seven country's defense budgets combined. At the same time the forces of behind-the-scenes subterfuge in the overturning of nations' leadership via backing would-be political clients of the U.S. moves apace.

In a sane and just world, the most salutary activity of a nation in the area of international relations is the promotion of peaceful coexistence among nations and cultures wherein benevolent, humane policy is valued over militant state power characterized by efforts to deescalate international tensions, coterminous with a respect and compassion for diverse cultures, religions and ethnicities. The use of economic standing as influence toward integrity, not predation and hegemony, is the best path toward a successful future for our world and the hard earned right to a position of leadership among nations. When the actions of a flagrant aggressor meet the criteria for U.N. involvement, then a military response may be prudently considered but only in the event of utter failure of diplomatic efforts and economic sanctions to avoid conflict. So many of the tenets of the Constitution and our founders rhetoric around the revolution speak to the dilemma we now find ourselves in as we enter the new millennium. The maintaining of both peace and prosperity are job one. We should think twice about being drawn into NPR style binary debates about most issues as if the "what were you wearing?" question were brought out at a rape trial. Rebuilding the U.S. nuclear arsenal to the tune of a trillion is the brain child of a government that clearly holds a dark second opinion on Nuremburg Principles.

The present day plague of mass killings on the home front is an inevitable "externality" of technofascism and its enabler, the military state. In fact, mass killings are technofascism made visible. The lethal rage coming from a deranged individual is roughly the same whether he is knife toting, baseball bat toting or assault rifle toting. Remember the multiplier effect of the attack on a civilian population from the air in Guernica? The simple fact of ordinance technology mapped on to murderous intent, which in this case was directed toward an innocent, non-aligned community, creates mass casualties beyond any previously imagined.

The intent involved in converting human beings to targets whether by a bombardier on an airplane or a sniper with a laser and scope is essentially the same. Dehumanizing flesh and blood into an image at a distance or in a scope, isolates the actor from the act and with it the direct experience of being an executioner or murderer.

Ask any medical examiner about the brutality of homicides. The victim of a strangling by hand is as great a proof of lethal intent as a two second spray of automatic gun fire coming from a freeway overpass. And of course the chronological age of competence in pulling and holding in a trigger is far lower than committing murder with one's bare hands. So at this writing, what we are now witnessing in the year of "mega-death" in America is both symptom and cause in the book. The flimsy argument that guns don't kill, people kill or only "insane" people kill is false on its face. All human aggression has a deranged component, but in a society in which weapons of mass destruction are exceedingly hard to obtain as in Australia for example, gun fatalities are at an all time low.

Where is the telltale-warning label on high-powered weapons: "any use of this weapon may cause injury or death"? Or how about, "hands off if you are insane." Dream on… And what happened to regulation? I'm talking across the board not just guns.

Were we to travel back a century or so, our mission: to inform the scientific community that their time honored tradition of embodying the vanguard of the evolution of our species, commonly known as progress, would one day lie under threat of science's junior partner, technology, we would get laughed out of the laboratory. Technology always was and is supposed to exist as practice and proof of scientific principles, not the other way around. Technology is a major wing of the engineering world; engineers "just do their jobs" in a philosophic vacuum. True, engineers in industry are not free to exercise their personal ethics for fear of being shown the exit door. Yet in truth, there is the exceptional engineer like Buckminster Fuller who maintains human benefit as the driver of innovation. As we survey world cultures as a whole, there are perfectly well adapted societies living off the land, burning wood, and calculating with their fingers, which are splendid examples of Darwin's seminal theory of evolution. For them science exists not as a body of knowledge so much as a body of instinct and codified tradition. Indeed it could be argued that when societies went out and conquered other societies, raping and pillaging, they mutated into a reckless, accelerated manifestation of natural evolution itself, and in so doing, falsely conflated the technology of war and destruction with a kind of evolutionary superiority that the poor islanders or so-called primitive peoples allegedly lacked.

Certainly throughout history, the power elites have feared and opposed great visionaries like Galileo and Copernicus. But never was astronomy meant to road test the telescope, nor were the laws of physics devised to get us to Mars. In the present era, science, and I mean unfettered, creative science, has never been so maligned, and so marginalized. In a sense technofascism might well have been predicted by Darwin himself as the sinister outcome of humans believing they could race ahead of evolution itself so to speak in their obsession with progress and in direct defiance of Mother Nature.

Another counter-evolutionary activity of our species is the organizing of almost everything into institutions and organizations. You are a citizen. You have a job. You are well educated. You attend church. Your vacations take place at Club Med. You keep your money in the bank. As for no-agenda time remaining in the day to build and experience nature's collectives such as family, immediate community, living sustainably on the land and exploring nature, we barely get to zero in the equation.

As a doctoral candidate at Harvard way back – at least it seems so now- in the twentieth century, in my love of the classical in art and music history, in composition, the notion of progress in artistic styles seemed to mean something somewhat different to me than to my colleagues and teachers. I simply failed to arrange western music into a progressive aesthetic hierarchy from medieval chant through the birth of atonality. Sick of the linearity of it all, I had come to believe that something about art and human imagination should remain a-chronometric so that a Mozart might be born tomorrow or some undiscovered composer in the 1600s turns out to have banished tonality and gone aleatoric on us.[1] When I place the last period on this discourse and set it aside, there is no telling what style of musical theme I might come up with. Timelines do not control time nor man. Nor do they help us ascertain the right thing to do in the moment including the moment when a species is about to obliterate itself out of addiction to technology.

... The Beginning

ENDMATTER

INTRODUCTION
Richard Rhodes, *Hell and Good Company* (New York: Simon and Shuster, 2014)
29-33
Hannah Arendt, *Eichmann in Jerusalem: A report on the Banality of Evil* (New York: Penguin Classics, 2006)

CHAPTER ONE: A CONSTELLATION OF DEATH STARS
1. Edwin Black, *IBM and the Holocaust, The Strategic Alliance Between Nazi Germany and America's Most Powerful Corporation* (New York: Crown Books, 2001) 7-15
2. Politifact.com, Promise Broken Rulings on the Obamameter (2017) partial source

CHAPTER TWO: CHAOS BY DESIGN
1. Sparknotes, www.sparknotes.com/history/american/spanishamerican/section2.rhtml
2. Sherry Salway Black, *Lincoln, No Hero to Native Americans* (D.C.: Washington Monthly, January/February 2013
3. Nancy Smith, Wasserman Schultz, "DNC Rigged The Primary, But the Judge Dismisses Law Suit Anyway" (*Sunshine State News.com*: August 27th, 2013)
4. *USA Today* www.usatoday.com/story/news/nationow/2014/06/05/ronald-reagan-

CHAPTER THREE: SUNKEN SHIPS DON'T LEAK
1. U.S. Government spent over $500M, www.independent.co.uk > News > World (London: 10/6/2016)
2. www.presidency.ucsb.edu, Statement by the President Upon Signing the "Freedom of Information Act." (July 4th, 1966)
3. www.goodreads.com/quotes/search?utf8=✓&q=foreign+wars&commit=- Search James Madison
4. "Jeff Bezos and Washington Post/CIA article," (12/18/2013) www.alternet. org/comments/media/owner-washington-post-doing-business-cia-while-keeping-his-readers-in-the-dark

CHAPTER FOUR: ALGORITHMS UBER ALLES
1. Mother Jones, www.motherjones.com/politics/2013/02/high-frequency-trading- danger-risk-wall-street/2/ (January 2013)

2. Ozer, www.academia.edu/11604620/Occurence_of_mercury_methylmer-cury_dioxin_and_dioxin-like_PCBs_in_fish

3. Shoshona Zuboff, *In the Age of the Smart Machine: The Future of Work and Power* (New York, N.Y., Basic Books Inc., October 2, 1989) 418-422

4. MordorIntelligence, www.mordorintelligence.com/industry-reports/indus-trial-robotics-market, (Hyderbad India)

5. The Editors of *Encyclopedia Britannica*, Moore's Law , online www.britannica.com/topic/Moores-law

6. *The Guardian*, "Our Minds Can be Hijacked" www.theguardian.com/tech-nology/2017/oct 05 /smartphone-addiction-silicon-valley-dystopia (London, 10/05/2017

7 www.ted.com/talks/tristan_harris_the_manipulative_tricks_tech_compa-nies_use_to_capture_your_attention/transcript?

CHAPTER FIVE : THE COUP, THE WHOLE COUP AND NOTHING BUT THE COUP

1. Jules Archer, Anne Cipriano Venzon, *The Plot to Seize the White House*, (New York: Skyhorse Publishing 2007) 25-30

2. Renee Parsons, Chronolgy of the Ukrainian Coup (*Counterpunch* March 5, 2014 www.counterpunch.org/2014/03/05/chronology-of-the-ukrainian-coup/)

3. Eric Draitser, "Leaked DNC Emails Confirm Anti-Sanders Conspiracy" (*Counterpunch* August 3, 2016 https://www.counterpunch.org/2016/08/03/leaked-dnc-emails-confirm-anti-sanders-conspiracy/)

4. Neil Sanders, *Your Thoughts Are Not Your Own: Mind control, mass manipula-tion and perception management*, (London, NumberSixDance Publishing, 2013)

CHAPTER SIX: SOCIAL MEDIA AS WHITE NOISE

1. Josh Fox, "The Arrests of Journalists and Film Makers Is a Threat to Democra-cy and the Planet," (New York, *The Nation*, April 6, 2017)

CHAPTER SEVEN: TECHNOFOODIST TAKEOVER

1. Vandana Shiva Editor, *Seed Sovereignty, Food Security*, (Berkeley, CA North Atlantic Books, 2016) 76-80

2. "Clinical and Laboratory Investigation of Allergy to Genetically Modified Foods," National Institutes of Health, Jonathan Bernstein, Principle researcher, www.ncbi.nlm.nih.gov/pmc/articles/PMC1241560/pdf/ehp0111-001114.pdf

3. The Future Control of Food: A Guide to International Negotiations and Rules on Intellectual Property, Biodiversity and Food Security 11-02-11 https://mu-noxfam.files.wordpress.com/2011/02/the-future-control-of-food.pdf

4. Betty Hallock , "To Make Burger, First You Need 660 Gallons of Water "(Los Angeles, *LA Times*, January 27, 2014)

5. Sara Murphy, "Coca-Cola and Nestle Are Sucking Us Dry Without Our Even Knowing It," (The Motley Fool), www.fool.com/investing/general/2014/03/02/coca-cola-and-nestle-are-sucking-us-dry-without-us.aspx (March 2, 2014)

6. Vandana Shiva, *Water Wars*, (Boston, South End Press 2016) 1-14

CHAPTER EIGHT: "FOR SALE BY OWNER" ON THE WHITE HOUSE LAWN

1. Philip Rucker, Hamburger, Becker, "How the Clintons went from 'dead broke' to rich" (*Washington Post*, June 26,2014) www.washingtonpost.com/politics/how-the-clintons-went-from-dead-broke-to-rich-bill-earned-1049-million-for-speeches/

2. John Kelly, Editor, *Industrial Relations, Critical Perspectives on Business and Management*,Volume II, (London and New York, Routledge, 2002) Chapter 22, 104-118

3. Carrie Brandon, Editor, *Issues For Debate In American Policy*, Eighteenth Edition, "Part 4. Environment, Drinking Water Safety" (Singapore, 2018) ISBN 978-1-5063-6880-1

4. Eduardo Galeano, *Upside Down, A Primer for the Looking Glass World* (New York, NY St Martins Press 2001)

CHAPTER NINE: "AROUND THE WORLD IN EIGHTY MEGATONS"

1. Saira Khan, *Nuclear Weapons and Conflict Transformation* (London and New York, NY 2009) 29-30

2. Albert Einstein, Brainy Quote www.brainyquote.com/authors/albert_einstein)

3. John Pilger, "Why the Documentary Must Not be Allowed to Die," (*Readers Supported News*, 01 January 7) http://readersupportednews.org/opinion2/277-75/47678-why- the-documentary-must-not-be-allowed-to-die

CHAPTER TEN: "ASSANGE AS HERALD ANGEL"

1. Telesur tv, (5 June 2016 - 07:02 PM), "For More Than 50 Years, CIA Went Deep into Ecuadorean Society" https://www.telesurtv.net/english/analysis/For-More-Than-50-Years-CIA-Went-Deep-into-Ecuadorean-Society-20160605-0028.html

2. Wikileals, (5 April 2010 10:44 EST), Collateral Murder, *collateralmurder. wikileaks.org*

3. Alex Seitz-Wald (2 May 2011 1:58 PM) "Flashback: Bush on Bin Laden" https://thinkprogress.org/flashback-bush-on-bin-laden-i-really-just-dont-spend-that-F-much-time-on-him-60cc2bd7af67/

4. Reuters, Jack Stubbs, Ginger Gibson (13 November, 2017) "Russia's RT America registers as 'foreign agent' in U.S."

5. *James W. Douglass, JFK and the Unspeakable* (New York, Orbis Books, 2013), Dick Russell, *On the Trail of the JFK Assassins* (New York, Skyhorse Publishing, 2008)

6. Peter Janney, *Mary's Mosaic* (New York, Skyhorse Publishing, 2012).

CHAPTER ELEVEN: "CHAPTER ELEVEN"

1. The Committee for Better Banks, (July21,2016) Wheeling and Dealing Misfortune   https://betterbanks.org/report/wheeling-and-dealing-misfortune-how-santanders-high-pressure-tactics-hurt-workers-and-auto-loan-

2. Bloomberg LP, Cecile Gutscher (2, February 2018 8:00 AM PST) "Subprime Auto Debt Is Booming Even as Defaults Soar" www.bloomberg.com/never-mind-defaults-debt-backed

3. Student Loan Hero (24 January 2018) "A Look at the Shocking Student Loan Debt Statistics for 2018" https://studentloanhero.com/student-loan-debt-statistics/

4. Maurie Backman (5 May 2017) This is the No. 1 reason Americans file for bankruptcy – https://www.usatoday.com/story/money/.../2017/05/05/...bankruptcy/101148136/

CHAPTER TWELVE: OCCUPY THE LANGUAGE

1. Science Daily (14 November 2008) Fish Choose Their Leader by Consensus https://www.sciencedaily.com/releases/2008/11/081113140310.html

2. The Young Turks with Bernie Sanders(23 May 2016) "CNN's Parent Company Among Top Hillary Clinton Donors" https://www.youtube.com/watch?v=1HpkGe-TGS0

3. Wikipedia(2007) https://en.wikipedia.org/wiki/Capital_punishment_in_Singapore

CHAPTER THIRTEEN: OBSTRUCT INJUSTICE

1. Online Library of Liberty, Editor John Bowring, author Jeremy Bentham (29 March 2018) The Works of Jeremy Bentham Vol IV , <http://oll.libertyfund.org/titles/1925>

2. Ibid

CHAPTER FOURTEEN: THE CONVENIENCE OF RUSSIA

1. Mark Landler and James Risen (25 July 2017) Trump Finds Reason for the U.S. to Remain in Afghanistan: Minerals

2. Robert Parry, (13 July, 2015)"The Mess That Nuland Made" https://consortiumnews.com//2015/07/13/THE-MESS-THAT-NULAND-MADE

3. K.T. McFarland (06 March 2016) Ronald Reagan won the Cold War… http://www.foxnews.com/opinion/2016/03/06/ronald-reagan-won-cold-war-But-it-was-nancy-reagan-who-made-it-happen.html

4. Wikipedia, https://en.wikipedia.org/wiki/Strategic_Arms_Limitation_Talks

CHAPTER FIFTEEN: WE THE PEOPLE ARE NOT AN AUDIENCE

1. Zhenhua Lu (28 March 2018) Thw White House has Hailed Kim-Jong-un's Beijing visit-but what are China's Intentions? https://sg.news.yahoo.com/white-house-hailed-kim-jong-il-231054722.html

CHAPTER SIXTEEN: TWISTED

1. Brainy Quote, Einstein: "You cannot simultaneously prevent and prepare for war" https://www.brainyquote.com/quotes/albert_einstein_137744
2. *Scientific American*, Larry Greenemeier (27 September 2011) "Something in the Way you Move: Cameras might soon recognize Criminals in Their Gait"
3. Katrina Selin (5 October 2017) World Socialist Website, Germany's Network Enforcement Act: Legal framework for censorship of the Internet, https://www.wsws.org/en/articles/2017/10/05/cens-o05.html

CHAPTER SEVENTEEN: DEMOCRACY NOW AND THEN

1. The National Security Archive (30 April 2001) Pentagon Proposed Pretexts for Cuba Invasion in 1962, https://nsarchive2.gwu.edu/news/20010430/
2. *Daily Kos* (07 July 2013) PBS And NPR: Subsidiaries of Koch Industries? https://www.dailykos.com/stories/2013/7/12/1223137/-PBS-And-NPR-Subsidiaries-Of-Koch-Industries

CHAPTER EIGHTEEN: REGIME CHANGE BEGINS AT HOME

1. Dominic Rushe (15 May 2014) FCC nears net neutrality rules as cable companies and activists feud, *The Guardian* https://www.theguardian.com/technology/2014/may/15/net-neutrality-fcc-open-internet-regulation-utility
2. AZ Quotes, Confucius, http://www.azquotes.com/quote/564510

CHAPTER NINETEEN: HIPPOCRAT OR HIPPOCRITE?

1. http://www.commonwealthfund.org/publications/issue-briefs/2015/oct/us-health-care-from-a-global-perspective
2. Brian Williams anchor, the NBC Nightly News (21 September 2006) Cancer docs profit from chemotherapy drugs, http://www.nbcnews.com/id/14944098/ns/nbc_nightly_news_with_brian_william#.Ws6PwBSOodc
3. Beth Mole (16 March 2018) Pfizer CEO gets 61% pay raise to 27.9 million-as drug prices continue to climb, ars TECHNICA, https://arstechnica.com/science/2018/03/amid-drug-price-increases-pfizer-ceo-gets-61-pay-raise-to-27-9-million/

AFTERMATH II

1. Chris Woodstra, Gerald Brennan, Allen Schrott Editors, *Classical Music, The Definitive Guide* (San Francisco CA, Backbeat Books 2005) 485

ACKNOWLEDGEMENTS

Those enablers who felt it too risky to be acknowledged in my book are now pronounced anonymous. I wish to thank my first writing partner and master of the felt tip note, the late Thomas Naylor, professor emeritus of economics at Duke University who rose to his full 6'4" as he shouted "Technofascism, that's a book we have to write!" Enduring gratitude goes out to professor, maven and mentor, Andy Farnell of the U.K., a wise and humane crusader in a proto-silicone world. No less do I wish to acknowledge my wife Antonia who, as if waiting ashore for her Magellan to round the horn, unfurling more sails than winds could fill, charmed my compass and tiller on course toward safe harbor.